MEN SPAKE FROM GOD

THE publication of this book in inexpensive paperback form makes available an outstanding contribution to the study of the Prophets of the Old Testament.

After an introductory chapter dealing with the function of the prophet and the nature of Old Testament prophecy, there are individual studies of the sixteen prophetical books, taken as far as can be determined in their chronological order. Each book is prefaced by an analysis; notes are given on authorship, historical background and so on; critical questions are discussed where necessary and an exposition of the main points of each prophecy is provided.

"Altogether," as one reviewer wrote, "the best conservative handbook on the prophets produced for many a long day."

Men Spake from God

STUDIES IN THE HEBREW PROPHETS

By

H. L. ELLISON, B.A., B.D.

*"Men Spake from God, being moved by
the Holy Ghost" (II Pet. 1 : 21, R.V.).*

THE PATERNOSTER PRESS

SBN: 85364 016 5

First Published, 1952
Second Edition, Copyright © 1958
Reprinted 1961
This Paperback edition, Copyright © 1966
The Paternoster Press
Second Impression, April, 1968

AUSTRALIA:
Emu Book Agencies Pty., Ltd.,
511, Kent Street, Sydney, N.S.W.

CANADA:
Home Evangel Books, Ltd.,
25, Hobson Avenue, Toronto, 16

NEW ZEALAND:
G. W. Moore, Ltd.,
3, Campbell Road, P.O. Box 24053
Royal Oak, Auckland, 6

SOUTH AFRICA:
Oxford University Press
P.O. Box 1141,
Thibault House, Thibault Square,
Cape Town

Made and printed in Great Britain for
The Paternoster Press, Paternoster House,
3 Mount Radford Crescent, Exeter, Devon,
England by Cox & Wyman Ltd., London,
Fakenham, and Reading

To

MY WIFE

who by her interest and steady encouragement
and cheerful shouldering of extra burdens
made this book possible
I thankfully dedicate it

CONTENTS

TO THE READER

THE conviction that the Bible is there to be read rather than to be read about is the only reason and justification for this book. But why then *this* book?

The Prophets mirror their own times with their problems so vividly, and they often express their thoughts so poetically, that some help is needed by the reader who has not had a theological training, if many parts are to be really intelligible to him. Then, too, the Church, not content with the many obvious Messianic prophecies, early took over the rabbinic maxim, "No prophet prophesied save for the days of the Messiah," and through most of its history has distorted what it could of the prophets to refer to Jesus Christ in His first or second coming, and has normally ignored the remainder, except for occasional texts, which were useful as pegs to hang sermons on. To take the Prophets simply and straightforwardly and to reap the spiritual reward of so doing is even to-day so difficult for many that some guidance is needed.

I have not written this book as an introduction to modern views about the prophets and their writings. There are quite enough books on the subject already. But certain far-reaching views on some of the prophetic books have become so widely known, at least by hearsay, that they could not be ignored, especially as they affect, whether accepted or rejected, our understanding of the prophetic message. Some will disagree with what I have dealt with and what I have omitted; probably all will disagree with some of my conclusions. As regards the former, I have learnt much from the difficulties of my own students; as regards the latter, though I have learnt from many, I have become the blind follower of none, and the only criticisms I shall regret are those based on the blind acceptance of the views of others however eminent.

In fairness to my non-technical readers I have given them the possibility in vexed questions of studying the views of others for themselves. The books mentioned in the footnotes have been chosen for the most part with an eye to whether they are likely to be available in libraries.

The chapters on the Major Prophets, and the Appendix, in their original form, first appeared as lessons in the Bible School of *The Life of Faith*. That they should have been expanded by the addition of chapters on the Minor Prophets is due mainly to the encouragement given by Mr. F. F. Bruce, Head of the Department of Biblical History and Literature, University of Sheffield, and Rev. H. F. Stevenson, Editor of *The Life of Faith*. Let this book be my expression of thanks. If I do not express thanks to others, it is not that I am not indebted to many, but to too many, and to have picked out some for mention would have been invidious.

The way in which this book has grown has inevitably involved inequality of treatment between prophet and prophet, with the longer prophets being the worst sufferers. I do not regret this. The shorter prophets are normally the least known and less has been written about them. In addition, if I interest anyone sufficiently to stir him to further reading, he is much more likely to spend money on a book to help him with one of the longer than one of the shorter prophets.

You will not really understand this book unless you read it with your Bible open at the same time, and you will understand it better if you use the R.V. I have only rarely pointed out the differences between the R.V. and the A.V., but have simply assumed that you would be using the former.

The Bibliography at the end is intended only to give you a list of books that may help in a deeper study of the text of the Prophets. They do not necessarily agree with my views and expositions.

The dates given may not agree in all points with the average reference book. They are based on the latest authority, P. van der Meer: *The Ancient Chronology of Western Asia and Egypt*.

I hope my more learned readers will not sniff at my use of "Jehovah." Though Jahveh, or Yahweh, whichever you prefer, is nearer to the real form of the name, it is not at all certain that it is the real form. So if I had chosen your preference, I should have sacrificed the very real spiritual connotation that Jehovah has for many without having achieved absolute accuracy.

It only remains for me to hope that your reading will bring you nearer to Him of whom all the Prophets spoke in sundry ways and divers manners, and that the ways and will of God will become more clear to you. If so, my work will not have been in vain.

NOTE TO THIRD EDITION

This paperback edition represents a careful revision in which as many necessary changes as were consistent with the publisher's needs have been made. It is hoped that in its new form the work will have even wider usefulness.

Moorlands Bible College, Dawlish   H. L. ELLISON.

LIST OF ABBREVIATIONS

a, b, etc.	Where only part of a verse is referred to, this is indicated by the use of one of the first four letters of the alphabet after the reference.
ad loc.	at the place.
A.V.	Authorized Version.
C.B.	Cambridge Bible for Schools and Colleges.
Driver LOT	Driver: *Introduction to the Literature of the Old Testament*—the page references are to the sixth and later editions.
Finegan	Finegan: *Light from the Ancient Past.*
G. A. Smith I or II	G. A. Smith: *The Book of the Twelve Prophets,* Vol. I or II.
HDB	Hasting's *Dictionary of the Bible*—5 vols.
ibid.	in the same place.
I.C.C.	International Critical Commentary.
ISBE	International Standard Bible Encyclopaedia—5 vols; an American work not easily procurable in Britain.
Kenyon	F. Kenyon: *The Bible and Archaeology.*
Kirkpatrick	A. F. Kirkpatrick: *The Doctrine of the Prophets.*
op. cit.	in the work previously cited.
LXX	The Septuagint; the oldest Greek translation of the Old Testament.
mg.	Margin.
N.B.D.	New Bible Dictionary
R.S.V.	Revised Standard Version.
R.V.	Revised Version.
Young	E. J. Young: *An Introduction to the Old Testament*—the best conservative introduction, almost unprocurable in Britain.

Also standard literary abbreviations and generally recognized ones for the books of the Bible.

CHAPTER I

THE PROPHETS

The Prophetic Books.

IN popular speech the Prophetic Books are the sixteen books of the Old Testament, from Isaiah to Malachi, and some would include Lamentations as well. They are further sub-divided into the four Major Prophets (Isaiah, Jeremiah, Ezekiel and Daniel) and the twelve Minor Prophets.

This enumeration and sub-division is not to be found in the Hebrew Bible. It is divided into the *Torah* (Law), *Neviim* (Prophets), and *Ketuvim* (Writings). The second section, the Prophets, consists of eight books: Joshua, Judges, Samuel, Kings (the Former Prophets), and Isaiah, Jeremiah, Ezekiel, The Twelve (the Latter Prophets). The reasons for the omission of Daniel, which belongs to the Writings, are considered in ch. XVII. For the moment it is sufficient to say that the rabbis made a correct distinction between normal prophecy and the apocalyptic visions we find in Daniel.

The distinction between Major and Minor Prophets is first found in the Latin Churches, and Augustine rightly explains that it means a difference in size, not in value.[1]

Though we are not dealing with the Former Prophets in this book, we shall profit by grasping the implications of books we call historical being considered prophetic.

The Functions of a Prophet.

The prophet is not defined or explained in the Old Testament; he is taken for granted. This is because he has existed from the very first (Luke 1: 70; Acts 3: 21), and has not been confined to Israel, *e.g.* Balaam (Num. 22: 5), the prophets of Baal (I Kings 18: 19). There are true and false prophets among the nations, as there are in Israel. But Amos makes it clear that the prophets of Israel are a special gift of God (Amos 2: 11) without real parallel among the Canaanites.

In the Bible, persons are called prophets whom we normally never call by that name, *e.g.* Enoch (Jude 14), Abraham (Gen. 20: 7), the Patriarchs generally (Ps. 105: 15). Moses is not so much the law-giver as the prophet *par excellence* (Deut. 18: 15; 34: 10).

[1] De Civitate Dei: 18. 29.

13

All this should prepare us for the realization that the popular conception of the prophet as primarily a foreteller is alien to the thought of the Bible. Indeed, the alleged antithesis of the Old Testament fore-teller with the New Testament forth-teller, should have saved us from this error. The two Testaments are not two books in opposition to one another, but two parts of the same book, and speaking the same spiritual language.

The best picture of the true function of a prophet is given by Exod. 7: 1f. The prophet is to God what Aaron was to Moses. When Moses stands before Pharaoh ("I have made thee a god to Pharaoh"), Aaron does all the speaking, even when the narrative might suggest otherwise, but they are Moses' words—Exod. 4: 15f, "Thou shalt be to him (Aaron) as God." In other words, the prophet is God's spokesman. Speaking for God may involve foretelling the future, and in the Old Testament it normally does, but this is secondary, not primary.

While the foretelling of the true prophet may normally be expected to come to pass (Deut. 18: 21f), that does not necessarily establish his credentials (Deut. 13: 1ff). Ultimately it is the spiritual quality of his message which shows whether a man is a prophet or not. In any case the foretelling of the future is never merely to show that God knows the future, or to satisfy man's idle curiosity; there is normally a revelation of God attached to it. We can know the character of God better now, if we know what He will do in the future. And as the future becomes present we can interpret God's activity the better for its having been foretold.

From this there follows that the prophet speaks *primarily* to the men of his own time, and his message springs out of the circumstances in which he lives. So some slight knowledge of the history and social background of the prophet are a help to the understanding of his message. But for all this, the source of the message is super-natural, not natural. It is derived neither from observation nor intellectual thought, but from admission to the council chamber of God (Amos 3: 7; Jer. 23: 18, 22), from knowing God and speaking with Him (Num. 12: 6ff; Exod. 33: 11). Though the ordinary prophet might not rise to Moses' level, and had to be satisfied with vision or dream, yet Moses' experience represented the ideal. We must beware of applying Deut. 34: 10 to all the written prophets. Though such a verse must by its very nature have been written a couple of centuries after the death of Moses, the latest date we can reasonably give to the final editing of the Pentateuch will be very early in the time of the united monarchy.[1] It

[1] See Aalders: *A Short Introduction to the Pentateuch*, p. 157.

cannot therefore be applied simply *a priori* to the written prophets, though possibly on other grounds some readers may wish to do it.

Since, then, the prophetic message is not merely a revelation of God's will, but of God Himself, it follows that it has a depth beyond the prophet's own understanding of it (I Pet. 1: 10ff), and that its significance extends beyond the prophet's own time, though its application at a later period may be rather different. In so far as a prophetic message is a revelation of the unchanging God, it has an unchanging significance. But none-the-less we will be better fitted to grasp its significance for us now, as we understand what the message meant to those who first heard it. Our study will, therefore, normally approach the prophets from this standpoint.

History as Prophecy.

We can now understand why Joshua, Judges, Samuel, Kings, are reckoned as prophetic books. The anonymous authors of these books—or it might perhaps be better to say editors—may well have been prophets themselves. At any rate they were given to see that the history of Israel was, in itself, a revelation of God. Their record of it sought less to give a history of the doings of Israel and more an account of the doings of God in and through Israel. This explains the stress on what the modern historian would consider non-essentials and the omission of apparent essentials.

This thought of Jehovah as the God of history permeates the Latter Prophets. The partial loss of this vision in our day has largely weakened the Church's preaching.

Early Prophecy.

In the historical books we are introduced to prophetic activity of a strange nature, *e.g.* I Sam. 10: 10–13; 19: 20–24. It is reasonable to attribute this partly to the baleful influence of Canaanite religion during the period of the Judges. However that may be, there is little, if any, trace of it in the written prophets. The wild men had degenerated into professional prophets, with their ecstasies and dreams (Jer. 23: 25), and are repeatedly condemned by the written prophets. Their last pitiful state is described in Zech. 13: 2–6. (The Messianic interpretation of Zech. 13: 6 is only possible by a gross neglect of the context.) Amos indignantly refuses to be called a prophet, if it involves his being classed with them: "I am no prophet, neither am I one of the sons of the prophets" (Amos 7: 14, R.V. mg.).

In contradistinction to these false prophets, the written prophets seem to have obtained most of their messages verbally—we cannot go further in our explanation than this—though we do meet with visions from time to time. As the prophets never really explain how the message came to them, it would be unwise for us to speculate too far on the subject.

The Form of the Prophetic Message.

The majority of the true prophets were bitterly unpopular —Ezekiel is apparently a major exception and there is no evidence for this after the exile. As a result, they could seldom rely on a large audience for any length of time. Their messages had normally to be packed into short pregnant form, generally in poetry, that they might be the more easily remembered. (The failure to indicate the poetic sections of the prophets is one of the major weaknesses of the R.V.; it could not be expected in the A.V. for they had not yet been recognized in the seventeenth century; this has been rectified in the R.S.V.) It should be remembered that before the days of printing, the only possibility of a message becoming widely known was for it to be passed from mouth to mouth.[1]

The best example of the prophetic message in its simplest form is given in Jonah 3: 4. We need not doubt that Jonah expanded it, whenever questioned about it, but basically this was his message. We find the prophetic tradition carried on by John the Baptist (Matt. 3: 2), and our Lord (Mark 1: 15).

The fact that the bulk of the earlier prophets and not a little of the later (not Daniel) is written in poetry should serve as a warning to us in our interpretation. It means that we are dealing not merely with the natural exuberance of Oriental language, but with the vivid metaphors and pictures of poetry as well.

At times the prophet became so unpopular that he could only gain public attention by unusual actions. Examples are Isaiah's vintage song (5: 1–7), and his going about dressed as a slave (20: 1–6). Jeremiah had to do this kind of thing a number of times: among them his remaining unmarried (Jer. 16: 2), his breaking of the bottle (ch. 19), his wearing a yoke (chs. 27, 28), his buying of land (32: 7–15), his use of the Rechabites (ch. 35), his hiding of stones in front of Pharaoh's palace (43: 8–13), his sinking of the scroll against Babylon in the Euphrates (51: 59–64). This element is very common in Ezekiel, *e.g.* his acting the siege of Jerusalem (ch. 4), the symbolizing of the scattering of the people (5: 1–4), the removal of his goods (12: 1–16), the rationing of his food (12: 17–20), his refraining from mourning (24: 15–27). It is the more remarkable here, as there seems to have been no necessity for it. It may be that such actions had come to be expected of a

[1] For the form of Hebrew poetry see Appendix, p. 150.

true prophet. The non-mention of such details in connexion
with the Minor Prophets may well be due to the virtually
complete lack of personal details in their writings.

The Shaping of the Prophetic Book.

Apart from Jer. 36, there is no indication given us how the
prophetic books were put together. It should, however, be
clear that the recorded prophecies cannot represent the whole
of the prophet's activities, even if we allow for frequent
repetition of his messages. The most obvious explanation is
that the prophet only preserved those of his prophecies which
best expressed the character and purposes of God, and would
best make them real to the future.

This probably explains why we have almost nothing of the
messages of men like Samuel, Elijah, and Elisha, preserved for
us. They were so intimately connected with the circumstances
of their own times that they had but slight importance for later
generations. We may be sure that the same was true of much
that the prophets dealt with in this book said. It does not
take any very close study to reveal long periods in their lives
from which we have few, if any, prophecies.

In most of the longer prophets the main guide in the putting
together of the prophecies preserved was spiritual connexion.
Chronology is not neglected, but it is obviously secondary,
and there are clear cases where it has been ignored for the sake
of spiritual connexions.

In Jeremiah's case we know from 30: 2, 36: 32 that there
were at least two collections of his prophecies in existence already during his lifetime. Isa. 8: 16; 30: 8 may well point to
something similar in the case of the earlier prophet especially
when we consider Micah's knowledge of him (see p. 63). Nothing
will really satisfy the evidence offered by Jeremiah, except the
theory that it was put together after the prophet's death by
Baruch. In ch. VI in considering the evidence for the authorship of Isaiah 40–66, we have had to assume the transmission
of Isaiah through a group of disciples, even though the book
may well have been given definitive form by the prophet before
his death. With Ezekiel there is every evidence that the
prophet looked forward to publication from the first, and that
it was he who shaped the book from first to last. A number
of the Minor Prophets give the impression that they were put
together by the prophet himself.

Unfulfilled Prophecy.

One of the major problems in the study of the prophetic
books is the problem of unfulfilled prophecy. The question
is normally shirked either by referring the fulfilment to the

B

Millennium, or by spiritualizing the prophecy and referring it to the Church.

The former method is seldom legitimate. Prophecies which refer to the last things normally do so quite unmistakably. There seems no justification for picking out others and making them do so too, just because we know that they were not fulfilled in the prophet's own time.

For the latter, there seems nothing to be said. Very many prophecies find a fuller meaning and fulfilment in the Church than they ever found in Israel. But this is by their having gained in *spiritual depth*. If a prophecy obviously does not refer to the Church in its primary meaning, its non-fulfilment in the prophet's time cannot be explained away by discovering a spiritual application to the Church.

Another school of thought minimizes the reliability of the predictive element in prophecy, and finds confirmation for its views in such unfulfilled prophecies, but this approach does not do justice to the facts.

The problem is really brought to a head in Ezek. 26. This is a prophecy of the complete destruction of Tyre by Nebuchadrezzar. Lest there should be any doubt as to its meaning, it is followed by a lamentation over Tyre (ch. 27), its prince (28: 1–10), and its king (28: 11–19). Yet Tyre was not captured and destroyed and its king killed. Sixteen years later (cf. 29: 17 with 26: 1) the king of Tyre was able to come to honourable terms. Ezekiel simply says that Nebuchadrezzar has had no gain from Tyre, but God has given him Egypt instead (29: 17–20). This is re-affirmed in the next chapter (30: 10 *seq.*). In spite of this, and Jer. 43: 8–13, there is no clear evidence that Nebuchadrezzar ever crossed the Egyptian border; he certainly never conquered the country.[1]

The very fact that Ezekiel neither apologizes nor explains in 29: 17–20 shows that he must have recognized a principle in prophetic fulfilment which we tend to overlook. This is probably to be found in Jer. 18: 7–10. Every prophecy is conditional, even when the condition is unexpressed. A prophecy of good may be annulled or delayed, if men do not obey, while repentance may suspend or reverse a prophecy of evil. We must make an exception when it is confirmed by God's oath.

It is only because we have the story of Jonah as well as his message that we have no difficulty with the "unfulfilled" prophecy of the destruction of Nineveh. Could we know all the circumstances, we should doubtless find similar circumstances elsewhere, where prophecy has not been fulfilled. The recording of such "unfulfilled" prophecies without explanatory

[1] Cf. H. R. Hall: *The Ancient History of the Near East*, p. 549. Nebuchadrezzar is the more correct form of Nebuchadnezzar.

comment is ample evidence that the prophet thought little of the evidential value of fulfilled prophecy.

For all this, "unfulfilled" is not in every case the best word; "suspended" would often be better. Nineveh was not destroyed in forty days, but some 150 years later it ceased to be a city. Nebuchadrezzar did not destroy Tyre, but the day came when it became a bare rock, a place for the spreading of nets in the midst of the sea. Egypt was never uninhabited for forty years (Ezek. 29: 11), but it has become a base kingdom, which has no longer ruled over the nations (Ezek. 29: 14f). Babylon did not sink like a stone in the Euphrates (Jer. 51: 64), but surely, slowly it went down into oblivion.

If this is so, he would be a very rash man who would maintain that the prophecies concerning Israel in Isaiah 40–66 are abrogated and not just suspended; that they have found their fulfilment in the Church, although it is obvious that much in these chapters cannot be referred to the Church by any strength of imagination.

A number of these points have been expanded in my *Ezekiel* e.g. the use of symbols (p. 32), the problem of false prophets (p. 51 seq.) and the conditional nature of prophecy (p. 102 ff.).

CHAPTER II

JOEL

THE STRUCTURE OF JOEL

THE DAY OF JEHOVAH

A. To-Day—Chs. 1: 2-2: 17.
    1—Ch. 1: 2-20.   The Swarm of Locusts.
    2—Ch. 2: 1-11.   The Approaching Day.
    3—Ch. 2: 12-17.   Effective Penitence.
B. The Future—Chs. 2: 18-3: 21.
    1—Ch. 2: 18-27.   Physical Blessing.
    2—Ch. 2: 28-32.   Spiritual Blessing.
    3—Ch. 3: 1-17.   Judgment on the Nations.
    4—Ch. 3: 18-21.   Final Blessing.

Author and Date.

NOTHING is known of Joel except his name and the obvious inference from his prophecy that he lived in Judaea.

The order of the Minor Prophets gives the impression that the scribes responsible for it aimed at approximate chronological order, modified where necessary by spiritual considerations. This creates a presumption in favour of an early date for the Book of Joel. From the internal evidence of the book itself we are virtually tied down either to a date early in the reign of Joash of Judah (*i.e.* shortly after 836 B.C.), or to one after the Exile—anything from 500 to 200 B.C. has been suggested.[1]

We do not consider either dating conclusively proved, and we here deal with Joel in his traditional position, for while the interpretation of the book is hardly influenced by its dating, its message underlies all written Hebrew prophecy.

The Day of Jehovah.

The Day of Jehovah, or of the LORD, is a fundamental concept in the Old Testament, never really introduced or formally explained. The Hebrew saw that the world does not show the perfection of God's rule, and that the righteous man does not fully reap the reward of his righteousness. The Old Testament does not look for a redress of this world's

---

[1] For the early date see Kirkpatrick, p. 57 *seq.*, HDB, article Joel, ISBE, article Joel; for the late date Driver: Joel & Amos (C.B.) or LOT, p. 308 *seq.* Young, p. 255 and N.B.D., p. 639 leave it open, preferring the former.

wrongs and sufferings in heaven, but expects God's intervention by which His sovereignty will be perfectly and for ever established on earth. This intervention with its accompanying upheavals and judgments is called the Day of the Lord (see also Amos 5: 18ff; Isa. 2: 12; 13: 6, 9f; Zeph. 1: 14f; Jer. 46: 10; Ezek. 30: 2f; Obad. 15; Zech. 14: 1; Mal. 4: 5).

Since any and every major divine intervention, especially when it involved judgment, not merely foreshadowed the final intervention and judgment, but also, for all that man could tell, might be its inauguration, the Day of the Lord is not used exclusively for the final intervention. This ambiguity has three main reasons, linguistic peculiarities in Hebrew, the real link between the foreshadowing and the fulfilment, and the revelation to the prophet of the nature of the Day of the Lord but not of its date in time.

The Swarm of Locusts.

The immediate cause of Joel's prophecy was an exceptionally severe invasion of locusts. Interpretations differ, some seeing here a description of the immediate past, others a prophecy of the future, but the most likely is that Joel speaks at the very height of the plague. After in ch. 1 describing the locusts and calling for a fast, for "the Day of the Lord is at hand," in 2: 1–11 he describes them in even more hyperbolical language, as they are seen against the lurid background of the Day of the Lord. So poetic and exaggerated does his language become, that many have found it impossible to believe that real locusts are here intended.

Allegorical interpretations of these chapters have been and still are popular; but quite apart from the complete lack of agreement as to how the allegory is to be interpreted, such an interpretation seems entirely unnecessary. The language, however exaggerated, can with few exceptions be suitably applied to locusts,[1] while the exceptions (2: 10f) are unsuited to human armies as well.

The prophet's lesson is that there are natural calamities so terrible and so surpassing the limits normally imposed by God, that they can only be explained as divine interventions in judgment. Whether or not such a calamity is inaugurating the final judgment is of little importance, for it is a guarantee that there is a final judgment.

The palmerworm, locust, cankerworm, caterpillar (1:4) are either different kinds of locusts, or more probably different stages in the development of the locust. Driver renders: shearer, swarmer, lapper, finisher.[2]

[1] See Driver: Joel & Amos (C.B.) *ad loc.* and especially p. 84–93.

[2] See Driver *op. cit.* and HDB and ISBE, article Locust.

The Giving of the Spirit.

Evidently the call to repentance and fasting was followed, for there is an immediate promise of Divine blessing (note tenses in 2:18f, R.V.). These verses (2: 18–27) refer to Joel's own time rather than to the more distant future.

Then there comes the promise that even as the judgment of locusts was followed by spiritual turning to God, so in the judgments of the Day of the Lord (2: 31f) there will be a tremendous outpouring of the Spirit. From the New Testament we know that this promise was fulfilled on the first Whit-Sunday (Acts. 2: 16). There is a tendency to suggest that this outpouring was not the fulfilment of Joel, but only a foreshadowing of the fulfilment in a day yet to come. This is not indicated by Peter, nor is it necessarily true. The coming of the Holy Spirit to found a body in which all barriers of birth, sex and social standing should be swept away, and in which the will and purposes of God should truly find expression is, in conjunction with the work of Christ, the supreme intervention of God in human affairs up to our time. The forty years that followed were the most catastrophic in their history for the Jewish people until perhaps our own time.

While the lack of perspective in the prophets' vision of the future is universally recognized, it is not sufficiently seen that the two comings of our Lord are inseparably connected, two phases of one great divine intervention. So the Day of the Lord looks not merely to our Lord's second coming, but to His first as well.

Unless, therefore, other evidence can be found, it would be dangerous to base any view of world-wide revival before the second coming of our Lord merely on this passage.

The Judgment of the Nations (3: 1–17).

For the average Israelite the Day of the Lord was first and foremost the day of divine vengeance on the enemies of Israel (cf. Amos 5: 18), therefore the prophets stress primarily the judgment on Israel (cf. I Pet. 4: 17), but the reality of the Divine judgment of the nations is never denied. It belongs to God's attributes as " Judge of all the earth."

The vision of judgment falls into two parts (vers. 1–8, 9–17), and the contrast between them is most instructive for our understanding of the prophetic picturing of the distant future. First Joel deals with nations known to him. Their treatment of God's people is to provide the ground of judgment, and as they have treated them, so will they be treated. Our Lord's teaching in Matt. 25: 31–46 lifts this to the highest plane and lays bare its underlying principles. Man's reaction to the people of God illuminates his true character and shows his true reaction to Christ Himself.

But there are other nations unknown to the prophet and to Israel. Immediately the sharp-cut details of vers. 1–8 vanish, and we meet the typical vagueness and general terms of apocalyptic (see p. 115). The prophet does not know on what grounds these nations will be judged, but he knows the judgment is certain.

It is likely that the valley of Jehoshaphat (vers. 2, 12) belongs to the symbolic language of apocalyptic. There is no certainty in its identification with the Kidron valley (though this is at least as early as the fourth century A.D.). Jehoshaphat means "Jehovah judges," and this is in all probability the reason behind the choice of name.

Final Blessing (3: 18–21).

All Old Testament prophecy sees in the final setting up of God's kingdom here on a transformed earth the goal of God's purposes; and this is echoed in Rev. 21, 22, where heaven is linked with earth but does not swallow it up or obliterate it.

There may be adequate reasons for anticipating an end of the material universe, and placing the eternal state in a purely spiritual "heaven," but they hardly justify the complete spiritualization of the Old Testament hope. The prophets' vision of a transformed earth was not merely the highest that they were capable of apprehending of God's purposes; it was also the vindication of God's wisdom and purposes in creation. There is no trace in the Bible of that depreciation of the material that came into Christianity from Greek philosophy and Eastern mysticism. While we must never forget that the unknown future can only be pictured in terms of the known present, we should yet hesitate to deny reality to the glowing visions of the prophets, and to affirm that this world is incapable of salvation and transformation in the cosmic stretch of the power of the Cross.

Joel's vision is limited to Judah and Jerusalem, not even the north of Palestine being included. It is quite understandable, then, that he sees only judgment and not blessing for the other peoples. This is one of the strong arguments for an early date for the prophecy.

CHAPTER III

JONAH

The Author and Date.

JONAH the son of Amittai prophesied during or shortly before the reign of Jeroboam II (782–753 B.C.—II Kings 14: 25). It should not, however, be taken for granted that the book was necessarily written by Jonah himself, as it is throughout in the third person.

The usual modern claim, based on linguistic evidence[1] reinforced by the almost universal unwillingness to accept its miraculous element, is that the book is post-exilic, and that it was written as a protest against the national exclusiveness of those that had returned from exile. We are far from convinced of the truth of the argument. We shall later show that the book fits into the needs of the middle of the eighth century B.C. We have insufficient evidence (only Hosea for certain) for the language of the North in the century before its fall to be dogmatic about the date of literature claiming to come from there. We agree with Sampey, "The Book of Jonah is anonymous, and we really do not know who the author was or when he lived. The view that Jonah wrote the story of his own disobedience and his debate with the merciful God has not been made wholly untenable."[2]

Historicity.

The uncertainty as to authorship need not affect our view as to the historicity and accuracy of the book; the oriental memory does not need to be tied to ink and parchment. If it was indeed written (and the same claim is made about Ruth) as a protest against the illiberality of the dominant spirit in post-exilic Judaism, it would hardly have had much effect unless it had been universally accepted as true.

Decisive should be our Lord's use of the book as historical (Matt. 12: 40f, Luke 11: 30). The appeal to our Lord's self-emptying (Phil. 2: 7, R.V.—the *"kenosis"* theory) is invalid, for He who had not the Spirit *"by measure"* would surely have been able to distinguish between history and parabolic or allegorical teaching, however noble.

[1] See Driver: LOT, p. 322, HDB, article Jonah.
[2] ISBE, article Jonah, The Book of.

Apart from the deep-rooted dislike of the modern spirit to accept the miraculous, there is no really valid argument against the historicity of the book. A man's unwillingness to accept the miraculous lies outside the scope of rational argument, and indeed our own willingness to accept is primarily an act of faith based on the resurrection of Jesus Christ, which in the last analysis we accept unhesitatingly because of what we know of Him. The other arguments against the historicity of Jonah are really arguments against an early date for its writing.

The Purpose of the Book.

Our estimate of the book's purpose will to some extent depend on the date we assign to its composition. Still it should be clear that the closing words are the climax of the book, "And should I not have pity on . . . persons that cannot discern between their right hand and their left hand; and also much cattle." Jehovah is not merely the creator of all life but its lord, and "He loveth all He made."

The idea that the early Israelites looked on Jehovah merely as a localized "tribal deity" has been largely exploded.[1] Their belief in Him as Creator was fundamental, even if its implications were often overlooked or forgotten. Jonah forgot one of them, when he tried to run away from Jehovah to Tarshish, and so earned for himself the stinging rebuke of the sailors (1: 9f). Just as the ordinary Israelite of the time attributed real, though perhaps vague powers to the gods of the other nations, so the sailors had quite understandably assumed that Jehovah was the god of the hills of Israel (cf. I Kings 20: 23).

Another implication was that Jehovah was the absolute lord of the nations, doing His will in and through them as He willed. But Jonah shows that this power was linked to a loving kindness which embraced all His creation.

This lesson of the power and love of God needed urgently to be learned in the middle of the eighth century B.C. In 745 B.C. Pul seized the throne of Assyria and called himself after one of the famous kings of the past Tiglath-Pileser (III). From then on Assyria was to be the rod of God's anger (Isa. 10: 5), smiting Israel until it ceased to be a people, and Judah until it was brought to the verge of destruction (Isa. 1: 9). In this time of unparalleled distress God's spokesmen had to see clearly that Jehovah was the lord of Assyria, and that behind all His smiting was His love. Where this truth was not grasped, the only logical course was to turn and worship

[1] Cf. Wright: *The Old Testament against its Environment*, p. 13.

the "victorious" gods of Assyria as did Ahaz and Manasseh (II Kings 16: 10–16; 21: 3).

The Sufferings of Disobedience (Ch. 1).

The wickedness of Nineveh needs no elaboration. The Assyrians seem to have been the only nation of antiquity in the Near East that gloried in cruelty, which they frequently depicted on their bas-reliefs.[1] A vivid impression of the hatred they caused will be gained from Nahum's fierce exultation over the coming fall of Nineveh. It is easy to understand why Jonah had no wish to save them from judgment.

In order to escape Jehovah's compulsion Jonah sailed for some port at the western end of the Mediterranean, the end of the world for him. (Ships of Tarshish were probably originally the ships that brought the metal ores for smelting; then the places called Tarshish would have got their name as main ports for the ore trade.)

There seems little point in stressing that neither the Hebrew nor the Greek (Matt. 12: 40) says that it was a whale that swallowed Jonah, for there are varieties that would have not the least difficulty in so doing. In actual fact we are left entirely in the dark as to what kind of marine monster it was.

The Psalm of Thanksgiving (Ch. 2).

This psalm is confidently appealed to as an added proof of the unreality of the story. It is said not to suit the circumstances (cf. ver. 5f) and to be a mere mosaic put together from other psalms (cf. the references ad loc. in any reference Bible); it is usually regarded as a later insertion. We agree that superficially at least the psalm is so incongruous, that its later insertion seems hardly reasonable. When, however, we grasp that Jonah is thanking God for saving him from drowning—hence the language of ver. 5f—which was for him a guarantee of God's forgiveness and ultimate deliverance, the psalm drops into place as entirely congruous. Even a land-lubber like Jonah knew that this was no ordinary fish.

As regards the language of the psalm, there are no direct quotations of other psalms, but rather echoes. Modern research has shown that the psalm of thanksgiving largely conformed to stock patterns, so such echoes are not entirely surprising, especially if Jonah, as was very likely the case, was attached to a sanctuary, where he may often have put together such psalms for the worshippers.

[1] There are some interesting examples in the British Museum.

Nineveh Repents (Ch. 3).

In the description of Nineveh there is probably an element of Oriental exaggeration, which is quite understandable. After the small tightly packed Palestinian cities on their *tells* the wide expanse of Nineveh, including even open land within its walls, must have seemed enormous. While "three days' journey" is a rough approximation, we find it confirmed for the circumference of the city by Diodorus Siculus, who estimated it at about 60 miles.[1] The impression—not necessarily correct—made by ch. 3 is that the whole of it took place within a day. If so the "day's journey" (ver. 4) covers his whole movements.

God's Tender Mercy (Ch. 4).

There came to Jonah the certainty that God had accepted the repentance of Nineveh (3: 10). It offended his sense of what God should do (4: 2), it spared Israel's most dangerous enemy, and though he did not say so, it destroyed his reputation as a prophet, so he asked to die (ver. 3). Still he decided to watch out the forty days in case God changed His mind (ver. 5).

His black spirits were slightly lightened by a gourd which grew up rapidly—"in a night" (ver. 10) need not be taken absolutely literally—and gave him a little shade. A worm at its root killed it and the hot sirocco wind both shrivelled it up and threatened Jonah with heatstroke. In his depression the loss of the gourd seemed the last straw. God was then able to bring home to Jonah through the importance to him of a mere ephemeral plant what God's creation must mean to the Creator. It seems likely that the 120,000 persons that could not "discern between their right hand and their left hand" are the younger children of two or three and under.

Additional Note.

The miracle of Jonah's preservation has more relevance than we might think. To the Israelite the untamable sea was a picture of chaos, the enemy of all settled order. Jehovah's control of the sea was also a picture of His control of chaos, and hence of everything. The great fish was doubtless a picture to Jonah of Leviathan, the monster lord of chaos, who meekly serves Jehovah as need arises.

[1] See Lanchester: Obadiah & Jonah (C.B.), p. 53. It is "Greater Nineveh" that is meant, the actual city was much smaller, see Bewer: Jonah (I.C.C.), p. 51.

CHAPTER IV

AMOS

THE STRUCTURE OF AMOS

A. **The Crimes of Israel and her Neighbours—Chs. 1, 2.**
    1—Ch. 1: 1, 2. Introduction.
    2—Chs. 1: 3-2: 5. The Crimes of Israel's Neighbours.
    3—Ch. 2: 6-16. The Crimes of Israel.

B. **Israel's Crimes and Doom—Chs. 3-6.**
    1—Ch. 3. Social Disorder.
    2—Ch. 4: 1-3. Judgment on the Women.
    3—Ch. 4: 4-12. God's Visitations in Nature.
    4—Ch. 5: 1-17. Inevitable Ruin.
    5—Ch. 5: 18-26. The Day of the Lord.
    6—Ch. 6. The Self-satisfied Leaders.

C. **Five Visions of Doom—Chs. 7-9: 10.**

D. **Final Blessing—Ch. 9: 11-15**

The Author.

SOME twelve miles south of Jerusalem on the brink of the drop down to the Dead Sea lay the fortified village of Tekoa,[1] near enough to the desert to bear its stamp, near enough to the high road up the backbone of the country through Beer-Sheba, Hebron and Jerusalem to know what was happening in the world. This was the home of Amos, who lived the arduous life of a shepherd (cf. Gen. 31: 39f). He may have been the owner of his flock, for the same technical expression is used of him and Mesha, king of Moab (II Kings 3: 4), *i.e. noqed.*

Amos offers us no indication of his spiritual history or of how God called him (but see p. 33). We can, however, from his prophecy recognize how he had been stamped in his thinking by the desert, where there is no place for half tones, for fine distinctions between light and dark, right and wrong. G. A. Smith is probably correct in suggesting[2] that Amos will have visited the towns of Israel on business, and that what he saw there must have created the certainty of Israel's doom in his heart. Then in rapid succession came the signs of God's wrath, drought (4: 6ff), locusts (4: 9; 7: 1), plague (4: 10—it ravished the Near East in 765 B.C.) and a total

---

[1] For a description of the landscape see G. A. Smith, I, p. 74.

[2] *ibid.* p. 79.

eclipse of the sun (5: 20—763 B.C.). It was clear to Amos that the coming doom was at hand, so he wrapped his cloak around him and went off with his message—"The lion hath roared, who will not fear? The Lord God hath spoken, who can but prophesy?" (3: 8). It was as simple as all that.

It is vital to realize that Amos represents something new in Hebrew religion. The indignant denial, "I am no prophet, neither am I one of the sons of the prophets" (7: 14, R.V. mg.) goes beyond the rejection of the idea that he prophesied for money. Once he finished his brief ministry in the North, he will have gone back to his flock, and he probably never prophesied again, *i.e.* he was never an official prophet at all. He represents that challenge to established form and order which has repeatedly been necessary to free the Church from the tyranny of tradition.

Though Amos' great successors could not have echoed his indignant denial, for they had known God's appointment as prophet, yet in their opposition to the "false prophets" and the official worship, in their long silences and their willingness to stand outside the normal framework of society they show that they had learnt the lesson of Amos' activity. The passage 3: 3–8 is particularly interesting as showing the spiritual compulsion behind his message.

The actual course of Amos' activity is not clear. It cannot have lasted long; it will have been cut short by the authorities, for in spite of the king's indifference Amaziah will have had the power to enforce his demands (7: 10–13). But it seems reasonably certain that his prophecy was given at the great autumn, *i.e.* New Year, festival at Bethel. It was probably spread over three days.

It may well be that it was Amos' prophecy of the coming earthquake (8: 8; 9: 5)—a prophecy fulfilled by one of the worst in Palestinian history (1: 1) for it was still remembered two and a half centuries later (Zech. 14: 5)—that stamped his message on men's minds and caused them to approach him with the request that it should be written down.

Amos' Message.

It will be no coincidence that Abraham, Moses and David all knew the wilderness, all had worked as shepherds, for under God this was a life that could teach a true scale of values. This was Amos' school in which he came to realize one of the foundation stones of true religion, that God was not merely just Himself, but demanded justice from men, and especially from those that worshipped Him. As preached by Amos it is over-simplified and gives a one-sided picture of God, but it was a foundation stone on which others could build. Until

He could reveal Himself perfectly in His Son, God's self-revelation had to be "in sundry ways and divers manners."

There was nothing intrinsically new in Amos' message. It breathes in the stories of Genesis, in the judgment of the Flood and of Sodom and Gomorrah, in Abraham's plea, "Shall not the Judge of all the earth do right?" and in God's commendation of him (Gen. 18: 19). It is made clear in the Book of the Covenant (Exod. 20–23, cf. 24: 4, 7), the fundamental law code of the people. The judge stands in the place of God, and to go to the judge is to go to God (Exod. 21: 6; 22: 8, 9, 28—cf. R.V. text and mg.). No distinction is made between civil and religious law, but the former is embedded in the latter. It is a leading feature in the teaching of the early prophets, *e.g.* I Sam. 15: 33, II Sam. 12: 1–15, I Kings 21 (note that Ahab's and Jezebel's judicial murder of Naboth was relatively a greater sin than all the Baal worship). Nothing alienated the affections of the people more readily from David than the suggestion, true or false, that he, God's representative, was not caring for the administration of justice (II Sam. 15: 1–6).

Amos does not analyse the reasons why this fundamental concept had been so largely ignored—that he was not exaggerating is shown by his later contemporaries Hosea, Isaiah and Micah—nor does he suggest reformations in religious and civil life which might result in increasing social justice. He demands the doing of justice as the only way of averting the otherwise inevitable judgment of God.

The Background.

As is almost universal in the prophetic message, Amos addresses himself to the rich and influential, to the rulers of the people. This is mainly due to the structure of oriental society, and to the fact that earlier Israelite religion, while never losing sight of the individual, did subordinate him to the community as a whole. It is our familiarity with the Psalter (and even here the community plays a larger role than we often realize) that often prevents our recognizing this fact. It is perhaps best demonstrated by Matt. 11: 5 where "and the poor have good tidings preached unto them" is given by our Lord as the clinching proof that He is the Messiah.

The sins he accuses them of group themselves roughly into three types. There are the gross violations of the ordinary decencies of life. Here come the crimes of the surrounding nations (1: 3–2: 3), gross immorality (2: 7b), inhumanity (2: 8a, cf. Exod. 22: 26f) and fraud (8: 5b). Then there are injustice, the perversion of justice and the luxury that leads to them. The only guarantee of justice in Israel was either the integrity of the judge or the power of one's own family and connexions. That is why the sad plight of the widow, orphan and stranger is so often stressed. God had entrusted the care of the weak and helpless into the hands of them that bore rule and judged (generally synonymous terms), and so injustice and the perversion of justice were peculiarly affronts to God (cf. Exod. 22: 21–24, 23: 1–3, 6–9). Amos' attacks on the luxury of the rich held nothing of the fox's rejection of the grapes beyond his leap as sour. Throughout the Bible period, and especially in the Old Testament, Palestine was an agricultural land with only those artisans that its internal economy needed. In such a society great riches could only be obtained by great wrong. The women's ornaments (Isa. 3: 16–23), the ivory couches and the eating of immature animals (6: 4), the drunkenness and indolence had all been made possible only by the grinding of the face of the poor and by gross injustice and perversion of justice.

The third group of sins includes all those acts that imply ignorance of or indifference to God's character and the privileges He had bestowed. Such were Judah's sins (2: 4), the rejection of prophet and Nazirite (2: 11f), a pretentious, hollow worship (4: 4f; 5: 21ff), and the ignoring of God's warnings (4: 6–11).

The main reason for Israel's moral condition was religious. It is dealt with especially by Hosea (see p. 37). Having conceived of Jehovah as merely their Baal, a god of the same type as the Baalim of their neighbours, they attributed to Him the capriciousness and non-moral character of the Baalim and assumed that the sacrificial ritual carried out with extreme elaboration and punctiliousness was the matter of prime importance to Him. Amos had the great gift of being able to put first things first. He did not ask whether the Northern sanctuaries were God-willed, whether the golden calf-images were a breach of the Sinai covenant, whether the ritual conformed to the divinely ordained pattern. He knew that reform along these lines would be and would remain external—examples are the abortive reforms of Hezekiah and Josiah. He knew that all the error came from a false conception of God, and that if the people came to a true conception of God, the other matters would reform themselves.

This is one of the chief lessons which Amos has to teach the Christian Church, for the tendency has at all times been strong to put correct Church order in the first place. But "correct" order is no guarantee of a "correct" knowledge of God, and still less of "correct" living.

The Crimes of Israel and her Neighbours (Chs. 1, 2).

The mention of all Israel's neighbours as ripe for judgment will have made the people think that the New Year was ushering in the Day of the Lord. Note that in at least one case (Moab, 2: 1 ff), and possibly in two others (Philistines, 1: 6ff, and Tyre, 1: 9f), the crimes condemned are not against Israel at all. God will not punish the nations because they have harmed Israel, but because He is the Judge of all the earth.

For the Nazirites (2: 11) see Num. 6: 1–21. Their purpose was obviously to enable the Israelite who had no other possibility of publicly serving God to show his zeal and love. The opposition to them arose probably from the Nazirites' rejection of the grape-vine and all connected with it, thus reminding the people of the contrast between the wilderness (cf. Hos. 2: 14f; 9: 10, Jer. 2: 2), where the covenant was first made, and the settled life of the land of Canaan.

Israel's Crimes and Doom (Chs. 3–6).

Amos' second message begins by stressing that not merely is God's justice even-handed—the inference from the first—but also that from him to whom much has been given, much is expected. Privilege implies responsibility. This is implicit in passages like Deut. 7: 6–11; 10: 12–17. Later prophetic passages repeat it, *e.g.* Isa. 40: 2b (see p. 56).

The passage 3: 3–8 is primarily a vindication of Amos' right to prophesy, but it is far more. It affirms that God's dealings with men follow consistent principles, which at least in general outline are understandable by men. The R.V. mg. in ver. 3 is correct.

The kine of Bashan (4: 1) are of course the rich women, living in luxury, who by their demands on their husbands encourage them in their oppression of the poor (cf. Isa. 3: 16–4: 1; 32: 9ff).

Since by the Deuteronomic legislation the third year was of special importance in tithing (Deut. 14: 28; 26: 12) and Elkanah's practice (I Sam. 1: 3, 21) suggests that the average Israelite concentrated on an annual visit to the sanctuary, which could be entirely independent of the three pilgrim feasts, it is reasonable to assume that 4: 4 represents the prophet's sarcastic exaggeration of normal custom—the A.V. is incorrect here. If so the use of leaven on the altar (4: 5 mg.) will not be a reference to a new custom in Bethel, but a continuation of this sarcastic exaggeration. According to Lev. 7: 13 leavened cakes were part of the sacrifice of thanksgiving, but they were not brought on the altar. If we have rightly understood the passage, 4: 4f is not a condemnation of the form of the Bethel ritual, but its rejection because for all its elaboration it was mere outward ceremonial. 4: 6–11 shows how empty it all was. The worshippers had not realized that the repeated calamities that had overtaken them were the best evidence that God had rejected their offerings.

Beer-sheba (5: 5; 8: 14) owing to its association with the Patriarchs had maintained its importance as a sacred place. For an Israelite to pass by Jerusalem to visit the unofficial sanctuary in the extreme south of Judah was an extreme example of will worship.

For the Day of the Lord (5: 18ff) see p. 20. The judgment of this Day cannot be averted by any ritual (5: 21ff)—the songs of ver. 23 are the psalms which even at this date accompanied the sacrifices, "the melody of thy viols" the musical accompaniment. The only thing that could avail was moral reformation (ver. 24).

The concluding verses of the chapter (5: 25ff) present major difficulties of interpretation, as may be seen by the LXX misunderstandings reflected in Stephen's quotation (Acts 7: 43) and in part in the A.V. rendering. Harper is probably correct in rendering ver. 25, "Was it only sacrifices and offerings that ye brought me in the wilderness during forty years."[1] Loving obedience was far more important than the sacrifices the people brought (cf. Jer. 7: 21ff and p. 85). In the next verse either the present (Harper) or the future (R.V. mg., Driver,[2] G. A. Smith[3]) is preferable to the past. Siccuth and Chiun (R.V.) are generally taken to refer to the Assyrian star-worship, which was becoming popular. If we take the verb as future, it means that the people and their idols would go into exile together.

Five Visions of Doom (Chs. 7–9: 10).

These visions, though told at the end of his public ministry, in all probability are part of Amos' call. Amos' message will have wakened fierce hostility not merely in official priestly circles (7: 10–13). So it is that in his second group of messages he had to give a general justification of his prophesying (3: 3–8), but now in his final appearance he had specifically to justify his message by an appeal to divinely given visions.

The visions contain a number of references to primitive ideas about the world, *viz.* the great deep (7: 4), the position of Sheol (9: 2), the great sea-serpent (9: 3). The force of the fourth vision (8: 1f) lies in a play on words; end=*qets*, autumn fruit=*qiats* (*cf.* Jer. 1: 11f, and p. 64).

---

[1] Amos and Hosea (I.C.C.), p. 136.
[2] Joel and Amos (C.B.), p. 192.
[3] G. A. Smith I, p. 171.

C

The sin of Samaria (8: 14) is generally taken to be the golden calf of Bethel—cf. "thy God, O Dan"—but on the basis of Hos. 8: 5f it is simpler to assume that a bull image was set up in Samaria as well, when it became the capital. This passing expression shows that Amos' virtual silence about the idolatrous, Canaanized worship of the North in no way implied approval or acquiescence.

Amos closes his message of doom by going beyond his earlier denial of Jehovah's favouritism (3: 1f). He not merely implicitly denies the commonly held view that Jehovah needed Israel, but explicitly affirms that essentially all peoples are God's people, and that all movements of the nations are as much God's doing as the Exodus from Egypt (9: 7). Therein lies the certainty that a just God will justly judge Israel. The A.V. mg. is correct in 9: 9, ". . . yet shall not the least stone fall upon the earth." God is not merely the God of the nation, but also of the individual, and ultimately His judgments are individual judgments.

Final Blessing (Ch. 9: 11–15).

These verses (or 9: 8c–15) are commonly denied to Amos, but the reasons seem inadequate. We agree that were we to picture Amos speaking these words in Bethel, it would imply an impossible contradiction with his previous message. But they will be the prophet's addition as he records his message for posterity. Nor is it fair to see a contradiction between the message of complete judgment in the prophecy as a whole and the promises of restoration here. However pessimistic a prophet might be about his own generation, he was completely optimistic about the future. Sooner or later God's purpose in the choice of Israel was bound to be vindicated.

There is hardly any contradiction between Amos' ethical position and the purely material picture here. A comparison with Joel 3: 18f suggests that he is using traditional language. Moreover if Isaiah consistently uses pictures of transformed nature as implying transformed men and that without formal explanation, it would be dangerous to assume that this was not traditional prophetic usage.

CHAPTER V

HOSEA

THE STRUCTURE OF HOSEA

A. Hosea and his Faithless Wife—Chs. 1-3.
    1—Ch. 1: 1-9. The Faithless Wife.
    2—Chs. 1: 10-2: 23. Israel's Faithlessness.
    3—Ch. 3. The Faithful Husband.

B. Jehovah and Faithless Israel—Chs. 4-14.
    1—Chs. 4: 1-5: 7. Like Priest Like People.
    2—Chs. 5: 8-6: 6. Fratricidal Strife.
    3—Chs. 6: 7-7: 7. The Testimony of History.
    4—Chs. 7: 8-8: 14. Israel's Political Unfaithfulness.
    5—Ch. 9: 1-9. The Corruption of Nation Religion.
    6—Ch. 9: 10-17. Original Sin.
    7—Ch. 10. Three Pictures of Coming Punishment.
    8—Ch. 11: 1-11. The Father's Love.
    9—Chs. 11: 12-12: 14. Israel False and Faithless.
    10—Ch. 13. Israel's utter Destruction.
    11—Ch. 14. Love Triumphant.

The Author and His Book.

ALL that we know of Hosea the son of Beeri is gleaned from his book. His prophecies themselves substantiate the inference to be drawn from the heading (1: 1), *viz.* that he started prophesying after Amos but some years before Isaiah (740 B.C.). Like Amos his message was addressed mainly to the Northern Kingdom, to which he undoubtedly belonged.

There is no strict order, chronological, logical or spiritual to be discovered in the major portion (chs. 4-14) of Hosea; the order even within the smaller subdivisions is often hard to follow; the unusually high number of marginal notes in the R.V. testifies to difficulties in language and text; the change from third person in ch. 1 to first person in ch. 3 is hardly compatible with the unifying hand of the prophet himself. In brief, it is quite likely that Hosea met a violent death in the last dark, violent and desperate anarchical years before the capture of Samaria, and that the book represents the treasured memories of one or more of his devoted disciples. This may also explain the relative absence of references to the major events of the time.

These factors make the book peculiarly difficult for closer study, but few of the prophets yield greater treasure—the use of the R.V. is particularly to be commended here. No other prophet comes nearer to the New Testament revelation of the love of God. This is the best explanation of the place of the book among the Minor Prophets. The scribes did not think him the earliest in time, and it is not likely that they were influenced by the length of the book. Chronologically Amos must always come before Hosea, the revelation of God's justice before the revelation of His love. But spiritually Hosea gives a deeper and truer revelation than Amos. So it was a true understanding that put Hosea first in order.

The Background.

The general background of the book is much the same as that in Amos, except that the social collapse which the earlier prophet foretold is now an accomplished fact. In addition the long shadow of Assyria now falls dark across the doomed land.

When we come to the religious background that which was only implicit in Amos here becomes explicit and dominating. It would be difficult here to give a satisfactory outline of Canaanite religion, the more so as much detail is still uncertain, but fortunately it is not necessary; only a few main points need to be grasped for the understanding of Hosea's message.

When the Israelites entered Canaan, they will have been struck at once by certain aspects of the religion of those they conquered. While Jehovah was the God of the people of Israel, the gods of the Canaanites were rather the owners of the land, and the gods of the people mainly because they lived in the land. While the interests of Jehovah and His demands from the people were chiefly ethical, the gods of the Canaanites were fertility gods governing the growth of vegetation and the crops with mainly ritualistic demands on their worshippers. While Jehovah stood uniquely alone in the worship of Israel, the minimum for the Canaanite was three, the chief god (a sky god), his wife (an earth goddess) and their son.

The prophetic writers never give us details of this religion. All the male gods are normally lumped together under the general name of Baal (pl. Baalim), which can be a proper name, but generally means lord or owner, cf. Baal-peor (Num. 25: 3, R.V. mg.), Baal-zebub (II Kings 1: 2), Baal-berith (Judges 8: 33) and a number of place-names compounded with Baal.

Equally the goddesses are referred to by the name of the most popular Ashtoreth or Ashtaroth (Babylonian Ishtar, Greek Astarte) or occasionally by that of Asherah (pl. Asherim or Asheroth—Asherah refers more commonly to the sacred pole in the Canaanite sanctuaries and is consistently mistranslated grove in the A.V.), cf. Judges 2: 11, 13; 3: 7.[1]

The first sign of declension after the death of Joshua was probably the admitting to honour of the old gods of the land to secondary honour beside Jehovah. This will have been followed by the far more serious step of worshipping Jehovah, as though He were merely a super-Baal, with the character, interests and claims of a Baal. For the prophets the worshipping of one's own conception of Jehovah is the worshipping of a false god, and so no distinction is ever drawn between the worship of the local Baalim beside Jehovah and the worship of Jehovah as a Baal. We can seldom be certain which is meant, the more so as they will have gone hand in hand, but probably the majority of mentions of Baal worship in the earlier books are really the worship of a Canaanized Jehovah. So far as the people were concerned they were probably never conscious of having forsaken Jehovah (cf. Jer. 2: 33).

Samuel and his sons of the prophets were probably the men who broke this religious degeneration, but how far it had gone may be seen by the names given in the families of Saul and David, who were certainly never Baal worshippers: Eshbaal, Saul's son, and Meribbaal his grandson (I Chron. 8: 33f; 9: 39f, cf. also 8: 30), Beeliada, David's son (I Chron. 14: 7)—cf. also Baal-perazim (II Sam. 5: 20), where Baal must mean Jehovah. Later scribes transmogrified these names to avoid the name of Baal, but the less read genealogies of Chronicles have preserved them for us.

With the division of the kingdoms, Canaanite influence increased in the North, especially during the attempt to introduce the worship of Melkart, the Baal of Tyre. Though this was defeated by Elijah and Elisha, it seems clear that the religion of the North became swamped by the Canaanite outlook. This is the background of Hosea, for while the worship of the Baalim he denounces probably included the worship of other gods, beyond a doubt it was primarily Baalized Jehovah worship, cf. 2: 16. As a result Jehovah was supposed to be primarily interested in sacrifice, not in conduct (see p. 31). Further, though the prophets never mention it for very shame, this Canaanized Jehovah must have been provided with a wife, and part of the worship will have been prostitution at the shrines, designed magically to increase the fertility of the

---

[1] An interesting picture of Canaanite religion has been given by the excavations at Ras Shamra, see Finegan, p. 147f., Kenyon, p. 158ff.

land (cf. 4: 14, where harlot=*qedeshah*, a holy woman, cf. Gen. 38: 21f, Deut. 23: 17, both R.V. mg.). This led in turn to wide-spread immorality (4: 14).[1]

Hosea's Wife (Chs. 1, 3).

Hosea's call came through God's command about his marriage (the R.V. mg. is preferable in 1: 2) and therefore presumably when he was a young man just out of his teens. The apparently natural interpretation of 1: 2, that he was commanded to marry an immoral woman, perhaps a *qedeshah*, though supported by many, can hardly be sustained.

i. Had Hosea known that Gomer was an immoral woman, there would hardly have been surprise or heart-break, when she returned to her old life.

ii. An immoral woman could not have served as a picture of Israel, when she came out of Egypt (2: 15; 9: 10).

iii. Since "children of whoredom" looks to the future, for they were not yet born, "a wife of whoredom" should do so too.

God will have commanded Hosea to marry Gomer, the daughter of Diblaim (the name is not likely to have any allegorical meaning). As the tragedy ran its course, Hosea will have realized God's purpose in His command and His foreknowledge of its consequence. So 1: 2 is the prophetic interpretation of God's command won through experience. The older view based on Jewish tradition was that the whole story is merely an allegory, but it has few advocates to-day.[2]

We cannot say how many, if any, of Hosea's children were legitimate, but the time came when Gomer left him for her lover. Either in sheer love or at God's command he did not divorce her—if he had, on the basis of Deut. 24: 1–4 (cf. Jer. 3: 1) he could not have taken her back. Then came the time (3: 1f) when he looked her up again and found her treated as a slave, perhaps sold by her paramour, who had tired of her. Hosea bought her back for one-and-a-half homers of barley, in value fifteen shekels of silver (translate in 3: 2, ". . . . even an homer of barley . . ."), *i.e.* half price as damaged goods (cf. Exod. 21: 32).

Though the prophet's message is God's word and he speaks for God, yet in ways we cannot grasp the message must first

[1] An interesting picture of debased popular religion has been given by the Elephantine Papyri, Finegan, p. 201, Kenyon, pp. 229, 275, Clarendon Bible, O.T. IV, p. 218.

[2] Young's advocacy of the allegorical view (p. 245f) seems to be based on a misunderstanding of the view set out above. For further details see HDB, article Hosea, ISBE, article Hosea, C.B. Hosea.

become part of the prophet (cf. p. 101). Nowhere in the Old Testament is the love of God more clearly and tenderly expressed than in Hosea, and that will be because no prophet experienced the heart-break of unrequited and faithless love as Hosea did. Hosea, like all God's messengers, had to experience his message before he could give it to others.

Hosea's Message.

Five points may be especially disentangled from Hosea's prophecy.

i. The immorality of Israel, using the word in the widest sense. It is clear that matters had become worse than in the time of Amos. Priests (4: 8; 6: 9), princes and king (4: 18; 7: 3) were among the ringleaders.

ii. The corruption of true religion especially as shown in the calf images (8: 5f; 10: 5f) and in the conception of Jehovah as a Baal.

iii. Lack of trust in Jehovah as seen in Israel's foreign policy (5: 13; 7: 11; 8: 9f; 12: 1; 14: 3). To seek foreign aid implied seeking the aid of foreign gods.

iv. For Hosea the very existence of the Northern kingdom was sin (8: 4; 13: 11). While it is true that God chose Jeroboam as a punishment for Solomon's sins (I Kings 11: 26–40), a careful reading of I Kings 12 will suggest a deeper hostility to the Davidic line than can be explained merely by high taxation; 12: 2f, suggest premeditated rebellion. Hosea looks forward to re-union under a Davidic king (1: 11; 3: 5).

v. The heart of Hosea's message revolves around the word *chesed*. This is found 247 times in the Old Testament, and is translated by mercy, kindness, loving kindness and eight other words of similar meaning. Though in many cases close enough, none of these terms really expresses the meaning of *chesed*, which is a covenant word, implying the loyalty and behaviour that may be expected from one with whom one stands in covenant relationship. Applied to God it means mercy and love, but it is always loyal love and covenanted mercies.[1]

Hosea's marriage was a covenant in which he had shown Gomer *chesed*, loyal love, but he was not shown the *chesed* by his wife which he had a right to expect. Even so Jehovah had made a covenant with Israel, had taken her as His wife, had shown her *chesed*, faithfulness and loving mercy, but Israel had not kept her side of the agreement. So He speaks through the prophet (6: 4) ". . . your *chesed* is as the morning cloud, and as the dew that goeth away early"; and then (6: 6):

[1] See further Snaith: *The Distinctive Ideas of the Old Testament*, Ch. V.

For I desire *chesed* and not sacrifice:
And the knowledge of God more than burnt offerings.

It is immaterial whether we render by love, dutiful love
(Cheyne), leal love (G. A. Smith), the meaning is clear; the
love of God to man will only be satisfied by the response of
man's love. R.S.V. renders steadfast love.

Hosea does not merely use *chesed* of God's love to man
(2: 19) and of the love that God asks of man, he also uses it of
the love He expects man to show his fellow-man (4: 1; 12: 6;
perhaps 10: 12). Since all Israelites were linked to God in
the one covenant, they were linked to one another too, and
part of the covenant keeping is loyalty between all who stand
within it.

Hosea and His Faithless Wife (Chs. 1–3).

The meaning of this section is made more difficult by faulty
chapter division in English and by a natural tendency to regard
ch. 2 as one connected prophecy.

Chapter 1: 2–9 is the story of Hosea's marriage up to the
point where it breaks down; ver. 7 is purely parenthetic. Then
the story is applied to Israel (1: 10–2: 23). Before the apparently
inevitable story of doom is unrolled it is preceded by an
almost incredible promise of restoration (1: 10–2: 1) with no
close link with what precedes or what follows. In ver. 10
"Yet . . ." is misleading; it is the simple "And it shall come
to pass that . . ." Then in ch. 3 we are shown from Hosea's
own action how God will carry out His promise.

The mention of pillar and teraphim in 3: 4, objects both
condemned by the Law (Exod. 23: 24; Deut. 16: 22; I Sam.
15: 23) does not imply the prophet's approval of them; he is
saying that every form of civil and religious organization, good
or bad, will vanish.

Jehovah and Faithless Israel (Chs. 4–14).

A foremost place is given to the priests' disregard of the
law of which they were made custodians (4: 6), as a result of
which "My people are destroyed for lack of knowledge."
Instead of restraining the iniquity of the people, they wel-
comed it for the sake of the resultant sin offerings—this is
the meaning of sin in 4:8; Hebrew used the same word for sin
and sin-offering, cf. II Cor. 5: 21, Rom. 8: 3. When we
remember that the priests were also judges, we can understand
better how terrible was their leadership in highway robbery
(6: 9).

A very old Jewish tradition maintains that the original
reading in 4: 7—changed by the scribes themselves out of

motives of reverence—was, "They have exchanged My glory for shame," *i.e.* for Baal worship.

Beth-aven (4: 15; 5: 8; 10: 5, 8) was a village near Beth-el (Joshua 7: 2, I Sam. 13: 5). Hosea transfers its name, meaning House-of-vanity, or House-of-iniquity, to Beth-el, which had ceased to be the House-of-God.

There are two references to contemporary happenings which we cannot now interpret. Harper (I.C.C.) gives no fewer than eleven interpretations of king Jareb of Assyria (5: 13; 10: 6) none of which carry real conviction—the R.S.V. is almost certainly correct in rendering with a different division of consonants, "the great king," *i.e.* the king of Assyria. There is also no certainty whether Shalman (10: 14) is short for Shalmaneser IV (782–773 B.C.) or even Shalmaneser V (726–722 B.C.), or whether he was an Assyrian king at all[1]; nor do we know where Beth-arbel was. It is references like these that remind us that we possess no more than the barest outline of Israelite history.

One of the most tragic features of Israel's history is her frequent superficial repentance. 6: 1–3 gives us a picture of one example. This section (5: 8–6: 6) is taken from the time of Israel's attack on Judah (Isa. 7: 1, 2; II Kings 16: 5).

Though he does not develop the thought, it would seem that Hosea's conception of Israel's history is much the same as that in Ezek. 20 (see p. 109), for he stresses that Israel's corruption began already in the wilderness at Baal-peor (9: 10, Num. 25) to continue from then on.

Even as in Hosea's own life love triumphed over sin and degradation, so his prophecy closes with the picture of Jehovah's love triumphant over Israel's sin (ch. 14). Few chapters in the Bible suffer more from the lack of inverted commas, for there are three speakers in it:

Hosea	vers. 1, 2	7	–	9
Israel	vers. 3	8a	8c	
Jehovah	vers. 4–6	8b	8d	

The division of ver. 8 is doubtful and difficult. If the above is correct, then "Ephraim" merely indicates the speaker of the following words, and "shall say" should be omitted.

How far this hope has been or will be fulfilled we cannot say (see p. 112f), but Paul quotes Hos. 2: 23; 1: 10 as one of his proofs of the triumph of the grace of God (Rom. 9: 25f) and goes on to the vision of the day, when "all Israel shall be saved" (Rom. 11: 26).

[1] See N.B.D., p. 1169.

CHAPTER VI

ISAIAH

THE STRUCTURE OF ISAIAH

A. **Assyrian background—Chs. 1-39.**
    1—(a) Ch. 1. **Introduction to section and whole book.**
    (b) Chs. 2-6. **Growth of obduracy in the mass of the people. (Chiefly time of Jotham.)**
    2—Chs. 7-12. **Consolation of Immanuel in the Assyrian oppressions. (Chiefly time of Ahaz.)**
    3—Chs. 13-23. **Judgment of the contemporary nations.**
    4—Chs. 24-27. **Judgment of the world and the last things.**
    5—Chs. 28-33. **The revolt from Assyria and its consequences. (Time of Hezekiah.)**
    6—Chs. 34-35. **God's avenging and redeeming.**
    7—(a) Chs. 36-37. **Deliverance from Assyria**
                (looking back.)
    (b) Chs. 38-39. **Entanglement with Babylon**
                (looking forward).

B. **Babylonian background. Chs. 40-66.**
    1—Chs. 40-48. **Deliverance from Babylon.**
    2—Chs. 49-55. **The spiritual deliverance of Israel.**
    3—Chs. 56-66. **The new Zion and miscellaneous prophecies.**

The Unity of the Book.

THE structure of Isaiah is unique. The first thirty-five chapters are attributed to Isaiah the son of Amoz, and are dated in the period Uzziah to Hezekiah. This first section, commonly called Proto-Isaiah by scholars—we use these names for convenience, not to prejudge the question of authorship—is closed by four historical chapters from the time of Hezekiah, which can be, but quite probably are not, from the pen of Isaiah. There follows an anonymous collection of prophecies (chs. 40–55—Deutero-Isaiah) in which it seems "the Babylonian Exile is not predicted; it is described as an existing fact."[1] The book ends with a less homogeneous section (chs. 56–66—Trito-Isaiah) in which the general picture seems to be the position after the return from exile.

[1] Kirkpatrick, p. 359.

The most obvious interpretation of these phenomena is that we have the work of one, or possibly two, anonymous prophets appended to the prophecies of Isaiah. Nor does the New Testament necessarily dispel such a view, for the attribution of passages from "Deutero-" and "Trito-Isaiah" to Isaiah *might* mean no more than that they were taken from the book which circulated under that name. The moment, however, that the phenomena of the book are examined more closely, the more difficult this apparently simple theory is seen to be.

We cannot here enter into questions of style, language and theology. It will suffice to say that the differences in these spheres between "Proto-" and "Deutero-Isaiah" are sufficient to suggest possible difference in authorship; the similarities demand some connexion between them.

Much more important is, that in "Deutero-Isaiah" we reach the climax of prophecy. After the picture of the Servant of Jehovah there was nothing more for the prophets to reveal about God, until the fulfilment Himself should come. It seems incredible that God could have raised up one in Israel to whom He could give such a revelation of Himself, and yet the messenger should leave neither name nor other trace in the traditions of his people.

Then, Isaiah is a literary unity, and a skilful one at that— cf. outline of its structure. The same arguments which would deny chs. 40–66 to Isaiah inevitably deprive him of considerable sections of "Proto-Isaiah." Furthermore, closer study has shown that there may well be sections by "Deutero-" and "Trito-Isaiah" in "Proto-Isaiah," and vice versa. In other words, to suggest that the work of a later prophet has been appended to that of an earlier one, is an over-simplification. If the unity of authorship is denied, then the only theory which does justice to the facts is that "a personal connexion between the three main parts of the book is found in the circle of disciples who handed down the Deutero-Isaianic material, and who had direct connexions with the Proto-Isaianic circle of disciples." [1]

When we consider the increasing complexities demanded by the usual modern view, and the many improbabilities it involves, it is surely easier to accept the traditional view of the Isaianic authorship of the whole prophecy. It must, however, be stressed that here, as in many other Old Testament problems, we are dealing with probabilities, not provable certainties. [2]

---

[1] Bentzen: *Introduction to the Old Testament II*, p. 114.

[2] For the unity of Isaiah see Young pp. 202–211, ISBE, article Isaiah, against HDB, article Isaiah, Driver LOT pp. 236–246.

The Problem of "Deutero-Isaiah."

We have already seen that the structure of Isaiah is unique. Once having accepted the Isaianic authorship of the whole book, we are not likely to question that Deutero-Isaiah was written in the dark days of Manasseh, when it seemed that true religion had perished, and the exile in Babylonia, prophesied by Isaiah to Hezekiah (39: 6f), became a necessity. With this dating agrees the form of the prophecies, which were probably from the first written rather than spoken. No open prophecy was possible in the time of Manasseh, and there is no reason to doubt the tradition that Isaiah suffered a martyr's death under this evil king.

But this is not sufficient explanation of the historical chapters which divide the book in two. They stand rather as a deliberate sign to the reader that we enter a new sphere of Isaiah's prophecy. If "Deutero-Isaiah" is by Isaiah, it is the one clear example in the Old Testament in which a prophet is transported from his own time, and not in fleeting glimpse, apocalyptic generalities or symbolism, but in clear vision is shown things yet far future.

We do not doubt that God could do this, but we may well ask whether He would. Is there a good reason for such an exceptional prophecy? We are of the opinion that there is.

Though the prophetic message is a revelation of God that comes from God, it has to come through the prophet, and God limits Himself by the prophet's ability to receive. This adaptation of the message to the personality and circumstances of the prophet is stamped on every chapter of the prophetic books.

We have already noticed that the figure of the Servant of Jehovah is the climax of prophecy. We may well suppose that God in His foreknowledge knew that there would be none of the generation of the exile spiritually capable of receiving such a revelation. It seems clear enough that Jeremiah would not have been able, for he does not seem to have come to an understanding of his own sufferings; and there is nothing to suggest that Ezekiel or Daniel was suited for the task. If that is so, we have adequate grounds for assuming that Deutero-Isaiah is in fact unique in its nature. (We shall see later that the figure of the Servant had to be set against an exilic background.)

The acceptance of Isaianic authorship explains one feature of "Deutero-Isaiah" that has puzzled those scholars who accept an exilic date for it, *viz.*, the vagueness of its geographical background. While the background of Palestine has grown faint, that of Babylonia has not become clear. This is what we might expect, if Isaiah were transported forward about a century and a half in time. (So vague is the background that some scholars have placed "Deutero-Isaiah" in Palestine of the exile, or even Egypt.)

One argument for the later date of "Deutero-Isaiah" is that, on the balance of evidence, it seems unlikely that it was known to Jeremiah, Ezekiel and other contemporary prophets. It seems fair to suppose that Jeremiah would have found his sufferings much easier to bear had he had the figure of the Servant of Jehovah before him to explain them at least in part. It would seem that though God gave the vision to Isaiah, He gave it for a generation yet future, viz., in the first place that of the late exile, and that this portion of the book of Isaiah was treasured up by the disciples of Isaiah (8: 16, see below) against the time when it would be needed.

Isaiah.

There is every evidence in "Proto-Isaiah" that Isaiah was a native of Jerusalem. As he seems to have had ready access to the royal court, and Ahaz evidently knew the name of his son Shear-jashub (this follows inevitably from 7: 3), he must have been a man of high social standing. The Jewish tradition that his father, Amoz, was the brother of Amaziah, the father of Uzziah, is attractive and quite possible. It is, however, too late to be accepted with certainty.

"Proto-Isaiah" covers the period from the death year of king Uzziah, 740 B.C. (6: 1, see below), when Isaiah received his call, probably as quite a young man, to at least Sennacherib's invasion, 701 B.C., and to even a later date, if there was a second invasion. This allows ample opportunity for Isaiah's writing of "Deutero-Isaiah" in his old age.

The Historical Background of "Proto-Isaiah."

During the reigns of Jeroboam II and Uzziah, Assyria passed through a phase of weakness and civil war; but when Pul, an Assyrian general, seized the crown in 745 B.C., five years before Uzziah's death, and adopted the title of Tiglath-Pileser III, it was the beginning of a new period of aggression and expansion which reached its climax in the conquest of Egypt and its end in the destruction of Nineveh itself (612 B.C.).

By 738 B.C. Rezin of Damascus, Hiram of Tyre, and Menahem of Israel had all become tributary to Assyria. In 735 B.C. Pekah, who had murdered Menahem's son, and Rezin raised the standard of revolt. They attacked Judah, presumably to force her into an anti-Assyrian alliance (7: 1f; II Kings 16: 5f; II Chron. 28: 5–15). In spite of Isaiah's efforts, Ahaz appealed to Tiglath-Pileser for help. In 734 B.C. the Philistine cities were captured. In 732 B.C. Damascus was captured and the inhabitants carried into captivity. Israel under Hoshea yielded at the cost of the loss of Transjordan and Galilee, whose inhabitants were carried away (II Kings 15: 29; 16: 9; I Chron. 5: 6, 26). Ahaz naturally became tributary.

An increase in Egyptian power encouraged Israel to revolt against Shalmaneser V, Tiglath-Pileser's successor (II Kings 17: 4). The inevitable result was the capture of Samaria in 722 B.C. by Shalmaneser, and the deportation of its inhabitants by his successor Sargon (II Kings 17: 5f).

At that time Judah had remained loyal to Assyria, but from 715 B.C. Egyptian intrigues increasingly inclined Hezekiah to revolt. Though involved in the revolt of the Philistines, Judah escaped apparently scot free in 711 B.C. (ch. 20); it may be that Hezekiah was able to yield in time. It is likely that the ambassadors of Merodach-Baladan (ch. 39) are to be dated between this and 701 B.C. Some scholars have, however, found evidence in Isaiah that Judah was invaded at this time.

When Sennacherib followed Sargon in 705 B.C., most of the Assyrian empire rose in revolt. Hezekiah was one of the leaders of the revolt in the west. Sennacherib was not to deal with the west till 701 B.C., but then opposition quickly collapsed. An Egyptian army was decisively defeated, and Hezekiah yielded, receiving very onerous terms (II Kings 18: 13–16).[1] Sennacherib, with a treachery he showed on other occasions as well, changed his mind and demanded the surrender of the city (II Kings 18: 17–19: 8; Isa. 36: 1–37: 8—cf. also Isa. 33: 1–12). This demand was not supported by any very great force, and was refused.

The more obvious interpretation of II Kings 19: 9–35 and Isa. 37: 9–37 is that Sennacherib, with his hands full, contented himself with writing a threatening letter, and the smiting of his host by the angel of the Lord led to his abandoning the campaign. Many, however, consider that there is a gap between II Kings 19: 8 and 9 (Isa. 37: 8 and 9) of rather more than ten years—this is quite compatible with the Hebrew method of writing history—and that Sennacherib had a second campaign in the west. The Assyrian records here are incomplete. For a full discussion see Bright, *A History of Israel*, pp. 282–287. It should be remembered that the results of Sennacherib's invasion were so disastrous for Judah that henceforth she remained a loyal vassal of Assyria.

Introduction (Ch. 1).

This chapter is not merely an introduction to chs. 2–12, but serves in that capacity for the whole book. It consists

[1] For the Assyrian version see Finegan, p. 177, Kenyon, p. 50f.

in all probability of a number of short, originally unconnected prophecies of varying date, but in the main probably from Hezekiah's reign, so arranged as to present God's "Great Arraignment" of Judah.

We find the assessors, heaven and earth, in ver. 2a—for God Himself is the judge; the charge is unnatural ingratitude (vers. 2b, 3)—the ox and the ass of the traditional Nativity pictures come from here. In vers. 4–9 we have the evidence for the prosecution; as the unchangeable character of God is assured, the blame for Judah's sufferings must rest on herself —the scene of utter desolation suggests the time of Hezekiah. Judah is imagined as pleading her regular and large-scale temple worship in her defence, but this is rebutted in vers. 10–17. As there is no other defence, the Judge makes a conditional offer of mercy in vers. 18–20; but vers. 21–23 imply that the offer has been rejected. The sentence, present judgment leading to purification and the restoration of a remnant, closes the chapter.

This chapter contains two of Isaiah's key thoughts, that of *holiness* and *the remnant*; these should be noted whenever they occur in the prophecy—see vers. 4 and 27 (her converts) and comments on ch. 6 below.

The condemnation of the Jerusalem temple-worship in vers. 10–17 should not be referred to the period of Ahaz' apostasy; it almost certainly dates from the time after Hezekiah's reformation. Note that so far from commending Hezekiah's action, Isaiah does not even mention it. Isaiah was fully aware that the reformation was purely external, and judged it accordingly. It is a painful thought to a certain type of "high churchman" that the main prophets from Amos to Jeremiah are unanimous that correct worship without corresponding morality of life only angers God, and is a sin. Indeed, the very correctness only magnifies the offence. It should be noted that the demand is for correct behaviour toward one's neighbour (cf. I John 4: 20).

This section is most instructive for the principles underlying the recording of the prophetic message. We may be certain that Isaiah repeatedly attacked the mockery of a purely external worship, but it is recorded only here and in 29: 13f. Once the message had been clearly given in the Introduction, posterity did not need its further repetition.

Judah under Jotham and Ahaz (Chs. 2–12).

Though, as has been indicated in the outline structure of the book, there is a break between chs. 6 and 7, and the two resultant sections are complete in themselves, yet they form a larger whole. Chs. 2–6 come mainly from the time of

Jotham, and depict the increasing hardening of Judah until there is no hope; chs. 7–12 are mainly from the time of Ahaz, and give the bitter fruit of the hardening.

We start with a picture of God's ideal (2: 2–5), possibly a quotation from an earlier prophet quoted also by Micah (cf. Micah 4: 1–5), which immediately changes to the grim reality (2: 6—4: 1). It should be noted that here, as elsewhere in the prophecy, present, future and final punishment all flow together under the general conception of the Day of the Lord (see p. 20f), although the expression strictly applies only to the final ushering in of the kingdom of God. The purification and final glory, which are the gracious result of the inevitable divine punishment, are pictured in 4: 2–6. The vintage song (5: 1–7) is both a condemnation of Judah's unnatural sin and an indication of Isaiah's difficulties. Unable to capture the ear of his wearied hearers otherwise, he goes round as a wandering minstrel at some vintage festival; note how cleverly the barbed point of the song is hidden until the very end. Six woes (5: 8–24) then indicate some of the "wild grapes" of the vineyard. Hard on their heels follow the Assyrians, the instruments of God's wrath (5: 25–30); when originally spoken this passage stood probably after 10: 4. Finally, Judah's hardness is explained by the story of Isaiah's call in ch. 6.

The second section begins with the rejection of the prophet's message and Jehovah's help by Ahaz and "the house of David" (7: 13) in favour of an appeal to Assyria (7: 1–25). This is approved by the people (8: 1–8). The prophet is denounced as a traitor, and turns his back on the people to devote himself to his disciples, who become a pattern for the remnant (8: 9—9: 1). A picture of the coming Messiah gives a gleam of light in the spiritual gloom (9: 2–7). There follows an oracle of judgment on Israel and Judah (9: 8–10: 4 and add 5: 25–30), and several on Assyria, threatening God's judgment when her work for Him has been done. The section closes with two Messianic chs. (11 and 12), which end with the fulfilment of 2: 2–5.

The Call of Isaiah (Ch. 6).

Many have failed to see the prophet's call here, and have looked on his experience as a sort of "second blessing."[1] There is nothing to be said for such a view; it only hinders our understanding of the prophet's message; it would seem to be based upon the failure to realize that in the Scriptures chronological order is always subordinated to the spiritual lesson to be learnt.

[1] So *The New Bible Handbook* and with hesitation Young, p. 213.

Isaiah was in the Temple court, in fact or in vision, probably at the great autumn feast celebrating God's sovereignty. The dying leper king symbolized to him the people's sinfulness. Now the worship of the seraphim brought home to him the sinfulness of the people's worship ("unclean lips"). The Israelite recognized that God was holy (*qadosh*), *i.e.* separate[1] from man, but understood it mainly physically, cf. Judges 6: 22 (R.V.), 13: 22; I Sam. 6: 19; II Sam. 6: 6ff. *et al.* (Obviously the people had to learn respect for God first). Now Isaiah realized that it was above all sin that created the barrier between man and God, though it did not exist for the earth. Note that Isaiah probably did not see the form of Jehovah, for the LXX and Origen are probably correct in interpreting "his face," "his feet" as referring to God. In any case, it was the glory of the pre-incarnate Son that he saw (John 12: 41).

This stress on the holiness of God runs right through Isaiah, especially in the phrase "the Holy One of Israel," which occurs twenty-five times in the prophecy, *including thirteen times in the second half.* (It is found in only six passages outside Isaiah, all probably later.) Not only is God holy, not only should Israel be holy, but God has separated Himself to Israel that He may be sanctified through Israel.

Isaiah's message is one of doom, for his task is one of hardening (6: 9f.). This passage is cited on three occasions in the New Testament, Mark 4: 11f (and parallels); John 12: 37–41; Acts 28: 25–28; and underlies the whole argument of Rom. 9–11. It should be clearly noted that the New Testament teaching is not that the hardening in part (Rom. 11: 7, 25, R.V.) came upon Israel because he rejected Christ, but that he rejected Christ because he was hardened (see especially John 12: 39).

In other words, it is from this moment that Judah ceases to function *as a nation* in God's purposes, though her national existence continued for over a century and a half. From now on, God is working out His purpose through a remnant, which is dimly seen in 6: 13. (This verse is unintelligible in the A.V.; see R.V.) The picture is of the tree of the nation hewn down, but the stock or stub left in the earth; from it new life can spring (cf. 11: 1).

We can now justify the position of ch. 6. It will only have been as Isaiah saw the people getting harder that he himself will have fully realized the implications of his task. Further, we can more easily understand God's action in the light of chs. 2–5. Though God hardens, there is an antecedent cause in the one hardened.

[1] See Snaith: *The Distinctive Ideas of the Old Testament*, ch. II.

D

Immanuel (7: 1–17; 8: 5–8; 9: 2–7, 11: 1–10).

Few who quote 7: 14 as evidence for the virgin birth of Christ trouble to study the promise in its context. The sign promised by Isaiah cannot be our Lord *in its primary fulfilment*. Isaiah has offered Ahaz any sign he likes that he may trust God, but Ahaz in mock piety refuses (7: 10–12). Isaiah then proclaims a sign. A maiden (*almah*) is about to conceive a son, who will be called Immanuel. Before he is about two ("Before the child shall know to refuse the evil and choose the good . . ." ver. 16) Rezin and Pekah shall be dead. Shortly after, however, Judah will have been wasted (ver. 15). Butter and honey are the food of a land where agriculture has ceased.

While this interpretation *and fulfilment* cannot be escaped, it is clearly a superficial one. The sign is a threat not merely to Ahaz, but also to the house of David ("The Lord Himself shall give *you* (plu.) a sign . . ." ver. 14). Immanuel is to be of the royal house (8: 8), and it is impossible to dissociate the child of 9: 6 from him. He cannot be Hezekiah, as claimed by Jewish tradition, for he was born some time earlier. Finally in 11: 1 he is definitely moved into the future, for the tree of David has been cut down, the shoot is out of the stock (R.V.) of Jesse, the branch is out of his roots.

While *almah* should mean a maiden, it is actually always used with the meaning of virgin in the Old Testament, and is therefore so translated in 7: 14 by the LXX and so quoted in the New Testament. *Betulah*, which should mean virgin, on the other hand does not necessarily bear that meaning, *e.g.* Joel 1: 8. So the use of an ambiguous word gives the sign a double meaning, one natural and immediate, the other supernatural and future.[1]

Maher-shalal-hash-baz (8: 1–8).

Immanuel was a sign for the king and royal house; Maher-shalal-hash-baz was to be one for the people. Note the method used to awaken curiosity. The strange phrase "Haste-spoil-speed-booty" is written on a large board and fastened outside Isaiah's house during the nine months his son is in his mother's womb. Only after the child's birth is it explained. It is clear that the prophet's appeal to the people had no more success than the appeal to the king.

Note that the identification of Immanuel with Maher-shalal-hash-baz, found in some commentaries, has nothing to commend it; also that the prophetess simply means the prophet's wife.

[1] See Lukyn Williams: *The Hebrew Christian Messiah*, p. 21ff, and E. J. Young: *Studies in Isaiah*, chs. 6 and 7.

The Rejection of the Prophet (8: 11–18).

While it is usual to praise Isaiah's clear-sighted foreign policy when Judah was attacked by her neighbours (7: 1–9), a very good case could be made for Ahaz' action from a purely worldly point of view. Certainly the people looked on it as the only hope of salvation and came to suspect Isaiah of being a Quisling (ver. 12, R.V.). The prophet himself seems to have lost confidence in his message for the moment (ver. 11).

The result was that Isaiah turned from the people and devoted himself to the small group that held with him (ver. 16ff). There is no evidence that he ever carried on a *regular* prophetic activity among the people after this, not even in the reign of Hezekiah; we gain the impression that he was given to intervening in moments of crisis. We must allow for the possibility that a good part of the following prophecies come from his teaching to his disciples, and we believe it was to them he entrusted "Deutero-Isaiah."

The Judgment of the Nations and of the World (Chs. 13–27).

Here, too, we have two sections organically connected. The oracles of doom on Israel and Judah could well raise the question whether God confines His judicial activities to His own people. To that, chs. 13—23 give an answer, for in them we see God's judgments on most of the peoples known to Isaiah, so these are really prophecies about other nations for Israel's learning, rather than prophecies for the nations' good. But that in turn leads to another question, *viz.*, was God's activity among the nations exceptional? This is answered by the apocalyptic and eschatological chs. 24–27. Here God's final judgment is seen to involve not merely Israel and the surrounding nations, but the whole world.

It is most instructive to note the difference in language between the two sections. In the former we have clear-cut pictures of the surrounding countries; in the latter we seem to be moving in a fog in which we see figures moving dimly until the sun of God arises in all its glory.

Delitzsch points out how the former section begins with Babylon, the city of world power, and ends with Tyre, the city of world commerce, while a second prophecy against Babylon forms the centre.

It is not clear why 22: 1–14, a prophecy about Jerusalem, is included in this section, but as Shebna was virtually Foreign Secretary, 22: 15–25 is entirely in place here.

The Taunt-Song Against the King of Babylon (14: 3–23).

This taunt-song (not proverb or parable, ver. 4) is one of the finest poems in the Old Testament, and must be interpreted

as poetry. A fine translation is given by G. A. Smith.[1]
It is not clear whether some definite king is here intended, or
whether Babylon is being personified in its king. In either
case, no reference to the fall of Satan is intended. Lucifer
(14: 12) simply means the morning star, and the application of
the name to Satan is due to patristic exegesis. At the same
time the king's overweening pride (14: 13) makes him a type of
Satan—"the Mount of congregation in the uttermost north"
is the home of the gods in Babylonian mythology.

Philistia (14: 28–32).

A logical *non sequitur* should be avoided here. "Out of the
north" (14: 31) shows that the prophecy has no connexion
with the death of Ahaz. The serpent, the basilisk and the
fiery flying serpent are Assyrian kings.

Moab (15: 1–16: 14).

There are two prophecies here, see 16: 13. It is not clear
whether the earlier, 15: 1–16: 12 is one of Isaiah's earliest, or
whether it is by an earlier prophet. 16: 1 implies a strong
ruler in Jerusalem who controls Edom. Uzziah is the last
king to satisfy the picture. It is equally uncertain whether the
earlier prophecy had been fulfilled at the time, or whether
Isaiah is saying that it is now to come into effect.

Egypt and Ethiopia (Chs. 18–20).

At this time Egypt was ruled by Ethiopian kings. Ch. 18
is addressed to the Ethiopian rulers; ch. 19 deals with the
Egyptian people; ch. 20 includes both in one common doom.
The interpretation of 19: 18–22 is far from easy. "The
language of Canaan" is Hebrew, and it probably refers to the
Jewish communities that sprang up later in Egypt. There
was a Jewish temple at Leontopolis from 160 B.C. to A.D. 72,
and its builders looked on it as the fulfilment, but this is
almost as doubtful as the identification of the great pyramid
with the altar and pillar.

In 19: 24f we have one of the finest universalistic passages
in the Old Testament. Though Israel still has the pre-
eminence in the use of "inheritance," the difference has become so small as to be virtually negligible; elsewhere "my
people" and "the work of my hands" are confined to Israel.

The Resurrection Hope (25: 6–8; 26: 13–19).

There is little clear teaching on the resurrection in the Old
Testament, this passage being one of the earliest. In 25: 6–8
we have the abolition of death for *all* peoples, but it does not

[1] The Book of Isaiah I, pp. 433–436.

extend further than the living at the setting up of the kingdom of God. In 26: 13f there is the guarantee that the oppressors of Israel are gone for ever, never to rise. But then in 26: 16–19 comes the promise that Israel's dead will arise. Further Isaiah was not permitted to see; and it seems that his contemporaries were not able to grasp his message (cf. 38: 18f). This may have been partly due to the obscurity of the language, partly perhaps to its restriction to his own inner circle.

Judah under Hezekiah (Chs. 28–33).

The general impression created by this section is that Isaiah did not resume his regular prophetic activity on Hezekiah's accession; most of these prophecies are called forth by the intrigues that led to Hezekiah's rebellion against his Assyrian overlord, and the consequences of his action.

The prophecies are divided into six sections by the word "woe"—28: 1; 29: 1; 29: 15; 30: 1; 31: 1; 33: 1.

The first woe is concerned with the dissolute nobles of Jerusalem. 28: 1–6 is an older prophecy by Isaiah against Ephraim applied in ver. 7f to the nobles of Jerusalem; ver. 9f is their drunken answer in broken Hebrew; ver. 11ff Isaiah's answer. 28: 23–29 should be read in the R.V.

The second woe deals with God's wonderful purpose for Jerusalem and the reception of the message by a hardened people. "Ariel" means altar-hearth, or hearth of God.

The third woe is uttered against the political intrigues with Egypt, and goes over into a Messianic picture.

The fourth and fifth are both concerned with the Egyptian alliance, interspersed with promises of divine aid and the Messianic transformation of society. 30: 21 is the great verse on guidance, which comes when men are going wrong, not while they walk right. 32: 3 reverses 6: 9f.

The last woe is addressed to treacherous Assyria, and once again ends in a glowing Messianic picture.

Judgment and Blessing (Chs. 34, 35).

Much of the message of "Proto-Isaiah" is summed up here. Edom personifies the hostile nations in general. That the eschatological picture should not be taken too literally is easily seen by comparing 34: 9f with 34: 11–15. A number of the beings mentioned in ver. 14 are mythological, but even they could not live in burning pitch and brimstone.

Ch. 35 is an outstanding example of the parabolic use of the transformation of nature so common in Isaiah, cf. also 11: 1–9, 40: 3f. etc. While there is no reason why we should not take the transformation of nature literally (cf. Rom. 8: 19–22), it should be clear that it is the antecedent transformation of men that is uppermost in the prophet's mind.

Historical Chapters (Chs. 36–39).

Chs. 36 and 37 obviously hang together, as do 38 and 39. The chronology of Hezekiah's reign is far from certain, but whichever we adopt, the fifteen years of 38: 5 would seem to bring us to a date before 701 B.C., the date of Sennacherib's invasion. Our knowledge of Merodach-baladan and his movements point in the same direction. Once we accept the Isaianic authorship of the whole book, Isaiah is just as likely to have influenced the order in II Kings as vice versa. In that case we have one more example of chronology being made subservient to spiritual ends. Chs. 36, 37 are placed first as rounding off the prophecies about Assyria; chs. 38, 39, though earlier in time, are placed last as looking forward to the captivity in Babylon to which 40–55 introduce us.

It is not easy to reconcile the general picture of Hezekiah in II Kings 18–20, II Chron. 29–32 with Isa. 28–33. Ch. 39 may help us. The resigned words of ver. 8 are not due to personal selfishness, content so long as trouble came later; they are rather the recognition of God's mercy by one who knew himself guilty. It is obvious that here we have one more example of the foreign intrigues that Isaiah denounced so unsparingly; but Hezekiah had gone into it with his eyes open. Even good kings like Hezekiah found prophets like Isaiah unwelcome at times.

The Historical Background of "Deutero-Isaiah."

Assyria has disappeared. Nineveh fell to the confederate armies of Babylon and the Medes in 612 B.C., and these two countries with Lydia formed a triple alliance dominating the Near East.

Jerusalem was captured and the Jews led into captivity in 587 B.C. Some thirty years later Cyrus, the Persian prince of Anshan—part of Elam, due east of Babylon (Isa. 41: 2)—was extending his power over Persia. Alarmed, Astyages king of Media attacked him in 550 B.C., but was betrayed into his hands. By 546 B.C. Cyrus had the whole of the Median empire under his control, and this brought him to the north of Babylon (Isa. 41: 25).

An initial attack on Babylon in 546 B.C. was quickly checked by the need to deal with Crœsus king of Lydia. He was defeated and captured in one short campaign, but Cyrus needed three years to subdue the Greek cities of Ionia.

Babylon was attacked in 539 B.C. The king, Nabonidus, "the first archaeologist," offered little opposition. The Babylonian army was routed in the field, and Babylon itself betrayed into the hands of the Persians. Only the citadel held out. This was stormed and Belshazzar, Nabonidus' son, killed (Dan. 5).

Cyrus gave the exiled Jews permission to return and rebuild the Temple—a permission which may well have been given to other deported peoples as well; but only a relatively small part, in which priests formed a high proportion, took advantage of the king's kindness (Ezra 1, 2). Obstacles and disappointments led to religious laxness, and these conditions may be reflected in some of the chapters of "Trito-Isaiah."

"Deutero-Isaiah" (Chs. 40–55).

Though it is comparatively easy to dissect Deutero-Isaiah (the approximate result is given by the paragraph divisions of the Revised Version), after the first few stages it does not often help very much in the understanding of the prophecy. Though these chapters form the closest unity of any prophetic message of comparable length, and contain a clearly marked progression in time, yet the thought does not develop along normal logical lines. We are not dealing with a unitary writing of the modern type, but with a series of prophetic poems, each complete in itself, yet all contributing to the building up of the final picture. This explains why, though "Deutero-Isaiah" contains some of the best-known chapters in the Old Testament, as a whole it is comparatively little known.

Though we are dealing with written rather than spoken prophecy, and the most sustained poetry in the prophetic books, the manner in which the message was originally received is obviously similar to that in "Proto-Isaiah." It would seem that the message in its totality only became clear to the prophet himself as he received and recorded it.

The Spiritual Background.

The universal belief in the Near East was that a god and his people were inextricably bound together. The god (or gods) needed his people as much as they needed him, for he needed the sacrifices they brought him—this view is violently attacked in Ps. 50: 7–13. The conquest of his people meant the conquest of their god by the god of the conqueror, and he was bound to fade away into impotence, starved as he was by the ending of his sacrifices.

Unless we grasp that this view was shared by a large majority in Israel, we shall not understand the shock of the Babylonian exile and the peculiar difficulties that Jeremiah and Ezekiel had to face.

Isaiah meets the resultant spiritual despondency with two

tremendous revelations of God, 40: 1–11 and 40: 12–31. The former is a message of comfort in which the main source of comfort is the very weakness of man (ver. 6ff). The deliverance is to be the work of God alone, and the assurance of it is based on God's Word. (One reason for seeing the end of "Deutero-Isaiah" in ch. 55, rather than in ch. 57, as in the older commentaries, is that thus we start with the Word of God going out in ch. 40 and returning to God in ch. 55: 11, having accomplished its work. A division after ch. 57 is based not on any intrinsic suitability, but on the similarity of 57: 21 with 48: 22, which does mark a major break.)

Fancy interpretations have been discovered for 40: 2b, but they can all be ignored. For anyone making a dispassionate comparison of national guilt and punishment in Israel and the nations, it would have seemed that Israel had suffered double in proportion to the others. "Quite so," says the prophet. God's "firstborn" may expect double, whether blessing or punishment (cf. 61: 7; Jer. 16: 18). The fact of the double punishment is proof that Israel has not been cast off, but is still God's firstborn; and so it is to-day!

The second is a hymn (40: 12–31) which is one of the most wonderful descriptions of God's power ever penned. The prophet's vision of His greatness, surely not derived from human speculation, is seen even more strikingly when we consider man's best concepts of God (ver. 18ff). A similar gulf exists between the Absolute of modern philosophic and liberal thought and Him who has been revealed as the God and Father of our Lord Jesus Christ. In the light of God's greatness, the despondency of the exiles (ver. 27) is absurd.

The Vindication of Jehovah.

By the destruction of Jerusalem and His temple, Jehovah had been humbled in the eyes of the nations. Now He summons them, that His honour may be vindicated (41: 1). For this He uses three witnesses or agents: Cyrus (41: 2–4, 21–29; 44: 24–45: 17; 46: 1–48: 16); Israel, His servant (41: 8–20; 42: 18–44: 5; 44: 21–23; 48: 17–22); and the Servant of Jehovah (42: 1–9; 49: 1–13; 50: 4–9; 52: 13–53: 12).

It will be noted that with the exception of the last three Servant passages, all these references are from chs. 40–48, which form a clear-cut section by themselves, and are commonly referred to as "The Book of Cyrus"; they deal with the deliverance from the Babylonian exile. In chs. 49–55 ("The Book of the Servant"), not only do Babylon and Cyrus disappear, but even in one sense Israel; now we read of Zion and Jerusalem, for the *spiritually* unredeemed people have now returned from their *physical* exile, or rather all obstacle to their return has been removed (48: 20, *cf*. with 52: 11f; 55: 12).

Cyrus was probably the first of those world conquerors who have swept meteor-like through the history of mankind, confounding every anticipation and inaugurating a new era in human history. Even if "Deutero-Isaiah" had been written by a contemporary, what a contrast its confident foretelling would be to the silence, confusion or ambiguity of the heathen oracles we learn of from Herodotus and other writers; how much greater is the contrast, if it was written a century and a half earlier!

Cyrus did not know Jehovah (45: 4f); this we know from his own inscriptions. From those of Darius I, we can infer with virtual certainty that he was a Zoroastrian who was polite to the gods of the countries he conquered.[1] If, then, he does Jehovah's will, he vindicates Him, for then assuredly the destruction of Jerusalem and the exile were Jehovah's doing (42: 24; 43: 28, A.V. and R.V. mg.). And as God's agent he is given a remarkable series of titles, unique in the Old Testament for a Gentile: My shepherd, *i.e.* My ruler (44: 28), His anointed, *i.e.* Messiah (45: 1), the man of My counsel (46: 11), he whom Jehovah loves (48: 14). But it is to be noted that no moral qualities are attributed to him; the titles are his not because of what he is, but simply because all unknowingly he carries out God's will.

Jehovah's vindication through Israel is seen not merely in their restoration, but far more by their becoming His worthy representatives (41: 8ff; 43: 4–7, 10, 12; 44: 21), although at the time they are slaves (42: 22, 24) and entirely unworthy of their call (42: 18–20; 43: 21–24).

The Servant of Jehovah.

With our lack of knowledge as to how the prophets received their message, it would be foolish to be dogmatic; but it does seem probable that the prophet only grasped the full implications of his message by degrees as it was given to him, even as we only understand it by degrees as we read it. So it is more than likely that Isaiah at first thought he was foretelling exactly that which would happen. But already in 42: 1–4 there appears the enigmatic figure of the Servant, who might be taken for Israel, and is yet so different from Israel. But with the jubilant call to Israel to leave Babylon (48: 20) there comes the realization that though Cyrus will do all for which he has been raised up, Israel will fail to carry out God's purpose (48: 22).

[1] For Cyrus' politic acceptance of the gods of Babylon cf, Finegan, p. 191, Kenyon, pp. 54, 141.

The Exodus from Egypt did not change Israel, and at the very Law-Mount they sinned, worshipping a calf of gold. The people whom the exile had not changed, would not be changed by the victories of Cyrus. Spiritual ends can never ultimately be attained by material means. So though Cyrus sweeps to his fore-ordained goal, there is no transformed Israel and so no transformed nature; then in 49: 1 the figure of the Servant slips out of the shadows.

The failure to realize the way in which the prophet's revelation developed, and the contrast between the glowing visions of Isaiah and the grim realities of the return, have made many conservatives deny that "Deutero-Isaiah" is primarily a prophecy of the return from exile; instead, they have applied it to the Church. To do so is to empty the prophecy of all coherent meaning, for while many portions can be applied to the Church, it is impossible so to apply the prophecy as a whole.

The traditional interpretation of the Servant has for many years now been denied by the vast majority of Old Testament scholars; usually he has been interpreted as collective Israel, real or ideal. This denial has not been due solely or even mainly to infidelity, as has been so often suggested, but rather to the reasonable conviction that the Servant could not be both Israel and the Messiah almost in the same breath.

The only tenable method of combining the traditional view with the general setting of chs. 40–55 was that of Delitzsch who wrote:

> The idea of the Servant of Jehovah . . . is rooted in Israel. It is, to put it briefly and clearly, a Pyramid: its lowest basis is the whole of Israel; its middle section, Israel not merely according to the flesh but according to the spirit; its summit is the person of the Redeemer. Or to change the figure: the conception consists of two concentric circles with a common centre. The wider circle is the whole of Israel, the narrower Jeshurun (44: 2), the centre Christ.[1]

One of the greatest gains of recent scholarship has been the very widespread recognition that the so-called Servant Songs (42: 1–4; 49: 1–6; 50: 4–9; 52: 13—53: 12) are a separate production from the bulk of "Deutero-Isaiah." This does not imply that they need be by a different author. It can easily be seen that if the Songs, and in two cases the connecting link, *viz.* 42: 5–9; 49: 7–13, are omitted, there is no apparent loss in sense. The effect of this isolation is to make a personal interpretation of the Servant almost compulsory, and the only personal interpretation that really satisfies is Messianic.

[1] An additional note in the German commentary on Isaiah by Drechsler and Hahn, 1857.

Professor North in his standard book[1] shows that Continental scholars have long been unhappy about the identification of the Servant with Israel, literal or ideal, but that the long list of individuals with whom he has been identified is equally un-satisfactory. We agree with him that only a Messianic figure in which kingly, priestly and prophetic traits are all blended does justice to the language of the Servant Songs.

The first Song contrasts the Servant's methods of action with those of the world, and even of Israel (41: 15f). Note carefully the R.V. mg. in 42: 3f.

The second gives a picture of the Servant conscious of the greatness of his task (ver. 6), but wearied by his long wait (ver. 4). Though fully fitted for the work, the sword is still in the scabbard, the arrow in the quiver. Here we have a picture of what the long "hidden years" in Nazareth must have meant to our Lord (cf. Luke 2: 49).

In 50: 4–9 we are introduced to the Servant in God's school, a hard school in which he was to endure "the con-tradiction of sinners." In spite of the attractive applicability of ver. 6, it is once again the years in Nazareth (cf. Heb. 2: 10, etc.) rather than the Passion that are under consideration.

Finally we have a vision of the perfect accomplishment of the Servant's work. It is indeed inadequate in its foreseeing of the resurrection, but otherwise it is the most perfect picture of our Lord's atoning work in Scripture.[2]

And so Zion, broken-hearted and despondent through the failure of the return, is transformed by the Servant; her Maker becomes her Husband, and the shame of her youth is forgotten.

The Servant and Israel.

In 49: 6 the Servant is called Israel, and this helps to explain why he and Israel both bear the title of Jehovah's Servant. The history of Israel is not merely the preparation for the coming of Christ. Jesus the Messiah is the fulfilment of all that Israel ever stood for in the purposes of God. Isaiah had experienced the failure of Israel and the choice of a rem-nant; looking out over the exile, he sees the failure there of the remnant (see especially ch. XIV). But beyond all the centuries of suffering and failure he sees one who is both Jehovah's Servant and the fulfilment of all that Israel had longed to be but never was. It is only through the anguish of the exile, and the failure of the return, that the prophet could be brought to this climax of vision.

[1] *The Suffering Servant in Deutero-Isaiah.* This is the most comprehensive modern work in English on the subject, and is of outstanding importance.

[2] For detailed study see David Baron: *The Servant of Jehovah.*

It may be noted that no effort is made to identify the Suffering Servant with the royal child, Immanuel, in "Proto-Isaiah." It may well be that Isaiah himself did not identify them, for until the Incarnation who could have imagined its stupendous wonder as God and man met in Christ Jesus?

"I create evil" (45: 7).

The many efforts to empty these words of their apparent meaning seem to be unnecessary and mistaken. They form part of an address to Cyrus, who was a Zoroastrian, a believer in a dualism in which light and good were the work of Ahura-mazda, darkness and evil of Ahriman. The context, therefore, seems to compel us to take 45: 7 literally as God's claim to be behind all that is. We do God no honour by putting the blame for sin and evil on Satan, for God is the creator and preserver of Satan, even as He is of men. In the light of the cross we need have no fear in accepting this, the extremest Old Testament statement on the sovereignty of God.

"Trito-Isaiah" (Chs. 56–66).

Unlike the two preceding sections of Isaiah, there is no coherent structure to be found here. Some chapters deal with "the Jerusalem that now is"; normally the picture seems to be of the post-exilic city, but sometimes the language is more applicable to the city of Ahaz and Manasseh, especially in its references to idolatry. Other chapters are eschatological. By a number of scholars chs. 60–62 are taken as belonging to "Deutero-Isaiah," with 61: 1–3 as another Servant Song. All we can do here is to indicate the various sections, adding a few comments.

Comfort to the Proselyte and Eunuch (56: 1–8).

In the rigorist atmosphere of the post-exilic community, probably some who had joined themselves to Israel during the exile found themselves no longer welcome; but Jehovah bids them welcome. When we consider that Daniel and Nehemiah (cf. Neh. 6: 11, esp. R.V. mg.) will have been eunuchs, we need not wonder at the presence of this message.

Venal Rulers and an Idolatrous Population (56: 9–57: 21).

While certain elements here might, on the basis of Malachi, be attributed to the post-exilic community, we have no suggestion that matters ever so degenerated, and for such open idolatry there is no evidence. It is better to suppose that it is the time of Manasseh that is depicted.

Sin and Redemption (Chs. 58, 59).

Here again we seem to be in post-exilic Jerusalem. First, the prophet deals with the apparently religious, before he turns on the open sin. During the exile, circumcision, Sabbath-keeping, and fasting were among the few open expressions of religion possible to the Jews; hence they grew in importance in the popular mind. Isaiah deals with the misuse of the latter two.

As might be expected, sham religion is accompanied by open sin, and the result is national disaster. The only hope is divine intervention.

"Arise, Shine" (Chs. 60–62).

There seems to be an inversion of order in these chapters (deliberate, by the prophet, not accidental in transmission). In ch. 62 we have a picture of continuous intercession for Zion, together with a fore-shadowing of what its result will be. In ch. 61 we have the Servant of Jehovah, who by his work brings it to pass, while in ch. 60 we have a picture of the glorious fulfilment, Whether these chapters belong to "Deutero-Isaiah," with which they seem to be linked by style, or not, they do seem to give the fulfilment of that prophecy. We are convinced that any effort to make these chapters apply only to the Church, instead of mainly to Israel, goes far toward emptying them of their full meaning.

The Day of Vengeance (63: 1–6).

The application of these verses to the Passion of our Lord is perverse, and is only possible by ignoring the sense of the passage.

A Prayer (63: 7—64: 12).

The prayer starts with the first person singular, but then changes to the first person plural. The prophet prays as the representative of the people. The development of thought is not easy, and observing the main sub-divisions may make its understanding easier. They are: 63: 7–10, 11–14, 15–19; 64: 1–7, 8–12. Note 63: 10, probably the only affirmation of the personality of the Holy Spirit in the Old Testament that is unmistakable without the help of the New Testament.

Final Blessedness (Chs. 65, 66).

Though in its original use ch. 65 will have had no connexion with the prayer that precedes it, it here stands as God's answer. The idolaters referred to are, once again, probably pre-exilic.

66: 3 is probably not a condemnation of sacrifice, either absolute or qualified. The end of the verse suggests that we have to do with those who combined idolatrous worship with their worship of Jehovah, and so their sacrifices became an abomination.

Note that the book ends, not with the new heavens and the new earth (66: 22), but with the carcases of the rebels. Isaiah is not only the prophet of the divine Redeemer, but also of human sin, which has made redemption through the Suffering Servant necessary. In the Synagogue, when this chapter is read publicly, ver. 23 is repeated after ver. 24 (cf. pp. 136, 154).

Note, too, how 65: 25 links with 11: 1–10, and implies the reigning of the king described in the earlier chapter.

Additional Notes.

The reasonable criticism has been made that the theory of authorship of "Deutero-Isaiah" given earlier implies that the same applies to "Trito-Isaiah." If that were so, it would seriously shake the theory, for there is nothing in chs. 56–66 to justify such an assumption. The term "Trito-Isaiah" is, however, a mere literary convenience. Part is almost certainly pre-exilic, part can be regarded as a portion of "Deutero-Isaiah" without any straining of probabilities, and the remainder is essentially timeless and is regarded as post-exilic mainly because of its setting in Isaiah.

There is a widespread idea in certain circles that the manuscript discoveries at the Dead Sea have disproved the composite authorship of Isaiah. The older MS: of the prophet must be dated about 150 B.C. If we accept the older view of composite authorship, it could only be disproved by a MS. earlier than 200 B.C. (cf. p. 124); that suggested on p. 43 would demand a MS at least as early as 400 B.C. before it could be rejected on these grounds.

More advanced students will find much of value in E. J. Young, *Studies in Isaiah.* The two chapters on *The Immanuel Prophecy* are of special value.

CHAPTER VII

MICAH

THE STRUCTURE OF MICAH

A. **The Coming Destruction of Samaria and Jerusalem—Chs. 1-3.**
    1—Ch. 1.   God's Anger against Samaria and Judah.
    2—Chs. 2, 3.   The Sins of Judah.
B. **The Messianic Period—Chs. 4, 5.**
    1—Ch. 4.   The Establishment of God's Kingdom.
    2—Ch. 5.   The Messianic King.
C. **The Controversy of Jehovah with Jerusalem—Chs. 6, 7.**

The Author and His Book.

MICAH, or Micaiah (Jer. 26: 18, R.V.), was a native of Moresheth-gath (1: 1, 14), as mall country town in the Shephelah, the low hills on the edge of the Philistine plain, near Gath.[1] While Isaiah depicts the social crimes of his time from the standpoint of the townsman in the capital, Micah shows us them from the standpoint of the suffering countryman. Nothing is known of him apart from his prophecies and the reference in Jer. 26: 18.

In the closing section of the book (chs. 6, 7) Micah's denunciations pass from the leaders to the people as a whole, and the general tone is much more gloomy than in chs. 1–3. There is a general tendency on the part of those who do not restrict (as some do quite unnecessarily) Micah's work to the first three chapters of the book to place the closing section in the dark days of Manasseh. This is quite probable, for the structure of the book suggests that these chapters are considerably later than 3: 12, which Jer. 26: 18 places in the reign of Hezekiah. In addition the picture given seems rather too dark for the reign of Hezekiah.

If this is so, it confirms the general impression created by the prophecy that Micah was a younger contemporary of Isaiah, outliving him in his public ministry. Micah contains numerous reminiscences of Isaiah,[2] though the most striking, 4: 1–5 (Isa. 2: 2–5), is probably due to common quotation from an earlier prophet.

If we have interpreted the evidence correctly, then we

---

[1] For a description of the neighbourhood see G. A. Smith I, p. 376ff.
[2] For a list see Cheyne: Micah (C.B.), p. 12.

must look on the heading (1: 1) as only approximately correct,
Micah's work beginning at the very end of Jotham's reign, but
going on beyond the time of Hezekiah.[1]

We get the impression that we have only a small portion of
his prophecies preserved for us, and that sometimes we have
the gist of his message rather than the original words in full.
The transition of thought is often violent, and in many cases
the only connexion between sections will be that of later juxtaposition because of spiritual connexion.   In places the thought
is made even more difficult by the possibility of dislocation in
the order of verses in transmission.

God's Anger against Samaria and Judah (Ch. 1).

The opening section (vers. 2–7) deals mainly with Samaria.
It is purely a message of inevitable doom, and therefore beyond her idolatry Samaria's sins are not specified.   As it now
stands the prophecy serves rather as an introduction to the
judgment on Judah, for Micah sees the Assyrian armies rolling
south over Judah and especially over the Shephelah, which he
knew so well, after Samaria's fall; so he raises his lament in
vers. 8–16.   This contains the longest sustained play upon
words in the Old Testament, the names of the places, probably
all in or near the Shephelah being chosen for that purpose.[2]   If
we are right in assigning this section to the reign of Ahaz, these
verbal fireworks probably reflect the prophet's unpopularity,
which forced him to such methods of gaining a hearing.   There
is no indication in the rest of the book that Micah was addicted
to puns.

The Sins of Judah (Chs. 2, 3).

Two groups of sins are particularly mentioned:

(a) The greedy landowners who covet their poor neighbours'
fields (2: 1–5) supported by cruel and venal judges and rulers
(3: 1–4), cf. Isa. 5: 8–24.

(b) False prophets (2: 6f; 3: 5–8) who support the rich in
their injustice and who use their position for their own gain.

The section closes with a drastic prophecy of the complete
destruction of Jerusalem (3: 9–12), which according to Jer. 26:
18f was the cause of Hezekiah's repentance, otherwise unspecified, unless perhaps in II Chron. 32: 26.   It is doubtful that it
refers to Hezekiah's reformation (II Kings 18: 4).

Though there is no reason for denying 2: 12f to Micah, the
verses break the connexion of thought very violently, and it is
likely that they have been misplaced in transmission.

[1] This is the attitude of ISBE, article Micah.   For the argument that
only chs. 1–3 are the work of Micah see in moderate form Driver, LOT, pp. 325–
334, and more strongly HDB, article Micah.

[2] For details see R.S.V. or Moffatt's translation.

The Establishment of God's Kingdom (Ch. 4).

There is no link logical or spiritual expressed as in Isaiah between judgment and the coming deliverance—even the "but" of 4: 1 is "and" in Hebrew. But there will not have been the need for his contemporaries. Though these chapters probably synchronize with chs. 1–3 rather than follow them, they are later in time than Isaiah's Messianic prophecies linked with Immanuel. The older prophet had struck the note which the younger could develop without the spiritual links of Isaiah's message.

The two prophets employ the earlier prophecy they use in common in similar but contrasting ways. Isa. 2: 2–5 is used as a contrast to the grim reality in Judah, Mic. 4: 1–5 as a contrast with the present heathen world (read R.V. mg. in 4: 5).

The following section is divided into three unconnected prophecies of deliverance and restoration, viz. ver. 6f; ver. 8ff; ver. 11ff. The mention of Babylon in ver. 10 has made difficulties for many, for why should Babylon be mentioned, when the enemy to be feared in Micah's day was Assyria? It is probably best explained by the element of dependence in Micah on Isaiah. The prophecy in Isa. 39: 6 is to be dated reasonably early in Hezekiah's reign (see pp. 46, 54), and a knowledge of it would explain the reference here. Naturally it is possible to explain it as a later scribal adaptation of the prophecy even as Stephen (Acts 7: 43) adapted Amos 5: 27; we do not, however, consider it likely.

The Messianic King (Ch. 5).

There is considerable difference of opinion as to whether ver. 1 should be taken with the previous chapter or with ver. 2 of the present chapter. The Hebrew includes it in ch. 4, but the general tendency is to preserve the present English chapter division (so R.S.V.) as against the R.V., which follows the Hebrew in its paragraphing. Cheyne (C. B.) is probably correct in regarding this verse as a separate prophecy acting as a transition from Ch. 4 to the thought of the Messianic king.

Apart from ver. 1 this chapter falls into a number of short unconnected prophecies, viz. vers. 2–5a (. . . this man shall be our peace); ver. 5b (When the Assyrian . . .)—6; ver. 7ff; vers. 10–15. The last of these, as not infrequently, pictures the Messianic age by the removal of the evils, social and religious, of the prophet's own time; ver. 10f implies the social evils that have arisen from increasing wealth and luxury.

The Controversy of Jehovah with Jerusalem (Chs. 6, 7).

The changes of thought here are even more violent than before. Any attempt to try and discover a connexion between

E

the various sections other than a general spiritual one is doomed to disappointment.

6: 1–8 introduces us to Jehovah's controversy with Judah, based this time not so much on the sins of the people as on their false conception of what He expects from them. The people are "wearied" by His service, an expression used in two other passages of the demands of the sacrificial worship on the people, *viz.* Isa. 43: 22ff, Mal. 1: 13. It is only our neglect of the legal portions of the Pentateuch and our failure to get a comprehensive picture of the demands of the sacrificial system as a whole against the economic background of the time that hinders us from realizing what a burden the system was, especially on the poorer man. In the days of Micah the tendency was to expand rather than cut down the ritual.

An appeal is first made to the time of the Exodus and the Conquest (ver. 4f), when the grace of God was supremely realized by Israel, but during which sacrifices and the ritual must have been cut to a minimum. "From Shittim to Gilgal" refers to the crossing of the Jordan; some part of the text has been accidentally dropped.

The misunderstanding people then ask how God is to be propitiated, suggesting an intensification of its sacrificial system (ver. 6f). The reference to human sacrifice is one ground for thinking of the reign of Manasseh (cf. II Kings 21: 6; Jer. 7: 31). Micah sums up the requirements of true religion in a famous verse (ver. 8), which virtually combines the teaching of his three great predecessors:

to do justly—Amos.

to love mercy, *i.e. chesed* (see p. 39)—Hosea.

to walk humbly with thy God, *i.e.* as befits His holiness—Isaiah.

In 6: 9–16 we have a second denunciation of Judah, but this time the stress is on social sin rather than false conceptions of religion. Israel answers God (7: 1–6, though this need not originally have been a unity with the preceding). In 7: 7–10 Israel still speaks, but it is now Israel of the future, on whom the judgments have fallen. Then the prophet answers her (7: 11ff), though the grammar suggests that the connexion is merely one of juxtaposition. The prophecy ends with a prayer (7: 14–17) and a doxology (7: 18ff).

With these notes of confidence the voice of recorded prophecy becomes silent for the rest of the long reign of Manasseh. God had spoken to Judah, but she would not hear. Now she had to sow the bitter seed that would yield a yet bitterer harvest.

CHAPTER VIII

ZEPHANIAH

THE STRUCTURE OF ZEPHANIAH

A. **The Judgment of the Day of the Lord—Chs. 1: 1-3: 8.**
   1—Chs. 1: 1-2: 3.   Universal Judgment focussed on Jerusalem.
   2—Ch. 2: 4-15.   Judgment on the Nations.
   3—Ch. 3: 1-8.   God's Judgment on Jerusalem.
B. **Universal Salvation—Ch. 3: 9-20.**

The Author.

THOUGH absolute certainty is unobtainable, there is a strong probability that the first of the true prophets of Jehovah to break silence after the reign of Manasseh was Zephaniah. There is virtual unanimity that 1: 4–9 must precede Josiah's reformation of 621 B.C. The only arguments against are based on "the remnant of Baal" (ver. 4) and "the king's sons" (ver. 8). But since the former may well mean "Baal worship to the last vestige," and the latter "the royal family" (the LXX actually has "the king's house"), we need hardly doubt the general impression made by this section of the prophecy.

There are grounds for thinking that it was the first tentative reforms of Josiah in 627 B.C. (II Chron. 34: 3; see p. 79) that were the external stimulus moving Jeremiah to prophesy, so it may well have been Zephaniah who a year or two earlier first stirred Josiah to his reforms.

Zephaniah, as is suggested by the local colour of his prophecy, obviously lived in Jerusalem, and he probably belonged to a family of some importance. This is suggested by his genealogy being carried back to his great-great-grandfather (1: 1). In no other prophetic book except Zechariah do we go further back than the prophet's father. On the other hand it seems gratuitous to assume, as is generally done, that his ancestor Hezekiah was the king of that name.

Universal Judgment focussed on Jerusalem (1: 2–2: 3).

For the conception of the Day of the Lord see ch. II. The contraction of the vision from a universal judgment to one on Jerusalem in particular is not unnatural. The Day of the

Lord, though universal, always centres around Israel. For the comparison of the judgment with a sacrifice cf. Isa. 34: 6.

RECONCILING BY MINIMISING DIFFERENCES The various religious offences mentioned are of great interest to the student of religions for the light they throw on the syncretistic religion that had grown up in Jerusalem in the days of Manasseh, but for detailed explanations a commentary must be consulted. We find the conditions under Manasseh reflected also in ver. 12. His policy of keeping on good terms with his Assyrian overlord, of which his religious syncretism was largely a result, will have created some measure of prosperity, while his flouting of the will of Jehovah and the message of the prophets passed without any very serious consequences for him or his people (but see II Chron. 33: 10–19— the history of Josiah's reign and passages like Jer. 15: 4 suggest that the repentance and reformation were very superficial). So, as always, the long-suffering of God produced the belief in some that God was indifferent as to how men acted (cf. II Pet. 3: 9).

It is widely held that just as Joel's vision of the Day of the Lord was inspired by the invasion of the locust swarms, so Zephaniah's was by the invasion of the Scythians. If, however, the opinion expressed in ch. XI (p. 81) is correct, this becomes improbable. After all we are dealing with the typically vague language of eschatology, where everything is seen through a haze of dust (cf. pp. 51, 115).

The corruption had gone too far for Zephaniah to share Joel's vision of a spiritual revival. He can only see the small number of humble (2: 3; better than "meek," cf. Mic. 6: 8), Isaiah's remnant, escaping the coming wrath (cf. Isa. 26: 20).

Judgment on the Nations (2: 4–15).

Since in the case of two nations no mention is made of sins at all, and in a third (ver. 15) it is only done in passing, it seems best to look upon this passage as a typical example of the Hebrew love for the concrete. The generalized language of 1: 2f is replaced by the mention of the Philistines to the west of Judah, Moab and Ammon to the east, Assyria to the north and the Ethiopians to the south. Ethiopia is chosen rather than Egypt, for like Assyria it is far away. So we have combined far and near and all the points of the compass, *i.e.* universality.

God's Judgment on Jerusalem (3: 1–8).

We have here the explanation why in 1: 2–2: 3 social sin and wrongdoing are hardly mentioned. However grievous the corrupt worship of Jerusalem, for Zephaniah the social injustice was worse, so it is dealt with as the climax of the prophecy of judgment. We find in ver. 6f an echo of the constant prophetic teaching that Jehovah is the God of all the earth; national calamity anywhere in the Near East should have been recognized in Judah as a sign that Jehovah was still reigning in righteousness.

Universal Salvation (3: 9–20).

Judgment on Israel is always linked, explicitly or implicitly, with ultimate restoration and blessing. This can only be denied by denying to a number of the prophets their promises of restoration (cf. p. 34). The judgment is never merely punitive, though it would be difficult to find Biblical support for the modern psychologists' objections to punitive justice. Here the principle is carried to its logical conclusion; also for the nations punishment has as its final purpose blessing.

While it is possible to justify both the R.V. text and mg. in ver. 10, neither is very convincing, especially as the prophecies of exile look normally to the North as the place of exile, and not Egypt. It is far more likely that there is a minor textual corruption, and that we should read with Ewald:

> Beyond the rivers of Ethiopia they shall offer Me incense,
> the daughter of Put shall bring Me an offering.

For Israel Ethiopia was at the ends of the earth; for Put cf. Nahum 3: 9.

There follows the picture of purified Israel (ver. 11ff). In ver. 12 "a humbled and weak people" best expresses the sense of the Hebrew.

The book ends with a picture of the redeemed people with the presence of Jehovah in their midst (vers. 14–20). The king of Israel is Jehovah himself (cf. Isa. 41: 21; Ezek. 34: 11). For the general picture cf. Isa. 12: 6; Ezek. 48: 35. Zephaniah must not be understood to be denying the reality of the Messianic king. It is hardly possible that any prophet conceived of Jehovah's direct presence except in the Shekinah glory, which had already been seen on Tabernacle and Temple (Exod. 40: 34; I Kings 8: 10f). Any more tangible presence implied a human representative, but not to mention him showed how perfectly he would represent Jehovah instead of obscuring Him as the earlier judges and kings had done.

CHAPTER IX

NAHUM

The Fall of Nineveh.

THE whole prophecy of Nahum revolves around the one thought of the coming downfall of Nineveh "the bloody city." It consists of a triumphal ode describing the power of Jehovah (ch. 1), followed by two pictures of the capture of Nineveh (ch. 2 and ch. 3).

The date of the prophecy can be fixed within fairly narrow limits. It must be after the sack of Thebes (No-amon; 3: 8) by the Assyrians in 663 B.C., and it must be before the actual fall of Nineveh in 612 B.C. The general religions situation in Judah hardly justifies our assuming a date earlier than Zephaniah (c. 627 B.C.), as does Kirkpatrick.[1] On the other hand 1: 13, 15 suggest that Assyria was still dominant in the West. Her power crumbled immediately after the death of Ashurbanipal in 627 B.C. We feel that the general tendency of moderns to place Nahum even nearer the fall of the city is based less on the internal evidence than on a widespread dislike to admitting more clear prophecy of the future than is absolutely necessary. The failure to mention the identity of the attackers in itself supports a date round 625 B.C.

Already in 626 B.C. Nineveh had been attacked by the Medes, but it was saved by the intervention of the Scythians. Some years later Babylon, which had become independent in 626 B.C. under the Chaldean Nabopolassar, joined hands with the Medes; they parcelled out Assyria's empire between them and attacked Nineveh, which fell in 612 B.C. Four years later the last vestiges of Assyria vanished unlamented, never to be revived.

The very vividness of Nahum's language and the splendour of his descriptions tend to hide from us his almost barbarous exultation over the doomed oppressor with never a word or suspicion of sympathy. It has its affinities with passages like Isa. 14: 4–21; Ps. 137: 7f; Rev. 19: 1ff. They reveal to us the awful lengths that man's cruelty and wrongdoing can reach; finally they dry up all compassion for the sinner in the deep satisfaction that God's justice has been finally vindicated. Nahum is so dominated by the sin of Nineveh that he makes no

[1] Kirkpatrick, p. 245ff.

70

reference to the sin of his own people—the only other prophet
of which this is true is Obadiah, and his is a special case (see ch.
XII).

The Author.

All we know of Nahum is that he came from Elkosh (1: 1),
an unidentified place, about which there are three traditions:

(1) It is claimed that Elkosh is the modern Elkush, a
village in Iraq about 27 miles north of Mosul, which is near the
ruins of Nineveh. Nahum's tomb is shown there, but the
tradition identifying it cannot be shown to be older than the
sixteenth century. Were this tradition correct, Nahum will
have been a descendant of one of the captives deported after
the fall of Samaria in 723 B.C. (II Kings 17: 6).

(2) Jerome (fourth century A.D.) was shown the hamlet of
Helkesi in Galilee by Jewish guides, who claimed that it was
Nahum's birthplace. We cannot now identify the site of this
hamlet with certainty. A barely possible support for Nahum's
Galilean origin is found in the name Capernaum=Kephar
Nahum, i.e. Village of Nahum. If this tradition is correct,
Nahum was the descendant of Israelites left in the North after
the deportations by the Assyrians (cf. II Chron. 30: 1, 5f, 10f,
18; 34: 6f).

(3) In a work known as the Lives of the Prophets, attributed,
perhaps wrongly, to Epiphanius (fourth century A.D.), a
native of Palestine, Elkosh is placed in the tribal portion of
Simeon, perhaps near Lachish.

Sentiment might make us favour either of the former views,
but we have to acknowledge that there is no real evidence in
their favour. Nahum's concern is clearly with Judah, not
Israel. The vast majority of scholars assume he was a
Judaean.[1]

A Triumphal Ode (Ch. 1).

Scholars have found an acrostic poem here, but the first
eleven letters of the alphabet can be discovered only by textual
manipulation, and the second eleven only by major alter-
ations.[2] There are two diametrically opposite errors connected with the Hebrew text that we must avoid. On the one
hand we must not assume that it has been handed down to us
in a flawless condition. Equally we must not assume that it is
full of major errors. All recent textual study, including the
evidence of the older copy of Isaiah among the Dead Sea

[1] One of the few modern writers to support the first view is Kirkpatrick,
p. 249 seq. Driver, LOT, p. 335, gives cautious support to the second view.

[2] There are 22 letters in the Hebrew alphabet. For details see HDB,
article Nahum.

scrolls, has supported a middle position, and there has been a strong reaction from the lavish textual reconstruction of an earlier generation.[1]

Though there are considerable textual difficulties in the first chapter, to suppose that an acrostic poem should have been so mutilated seems impossible, unless we say of the writer with Pfeiffer, "It is clear that he did not copy the alphabetic psalm from a manuscript but wrote it down as best he could from memory. He had not only forgotten the second part of this poem, but being unconscious of the alphabetic arrangement of the lines, he paraphrased certain lines . . ." [2] Faced with this, common sense is likely to decide that the few indications of an acrostic are purely accidental.

The ode begins with a description of the attributes of Jehovah (vers. 2, 3a) and of His power in nature (vers. 3b–6), both of which justify the confidence that He will at last carry out the punishment of Assyria first pronounced by Jonah (Jonah 3: 4) and affirmed clearly by Isaiah (Isa. 10: 12, 16–19, etc.). Then comes the promise (vers. 7–15) that Jehovah will make an end of the enemies of His people. There are textual corruptions in vers. 10 and 12; the verbs in ver. 11 should be in the past, for the verse probably refers to Sennacherib; in ver. 12 the R.V. mg. should be followed. To get the sense we should omit 1: 13, 15; 2: 2, for while we do not doubt that they are by Nahum, in their present setting, addressed as they are to Judah, they interrupt the address to Assyria. This is particularly true of 2: 2.

The Siege and Fall of Nineveh (Chs. 2, 3).

The chapter division is correct, for we have two poems on the same subject. Nahum is not giving a vision of the actual capture of Nineveh, nor does he give a detailed description of the siege. He gives a vivid series of pictures of ancient siege warfare as such sieges always were. Nineveh was doomed and it was in this way that she would go down into silence.

[1] See especially B. J. Roberts: *The Old Testament Text and Versions*.

[2] *Introduction to the Old Testament*, p. 595.

CHAPTER X

HABAKKUK

THE STRUCTURE OF HABAKKUK

A. A Spiritual Dialogue—Chs. 1, 2.
    1—1: 2ff. The Prophet's Complaint.
    2—1: 5-11. God's Answer.
    3—1: 12-17. The Prophet's Protest.
    4—2: 1-5. God's Answer.
    5—2: 6-20. Five Woes against the Chaldeans.
        (a) ver. 6ff. Their Conquests.
        (b) ver. 9ff. Their Rapacity.
        (c) ver. 12ff. Their Oppression of the Conquered.
        (d) ver. 15ff. Their Humiliation of the Conquered.
        (e) ver. 18ff. Their idolatry.
B. A Psalm of God's Intervention—Ch. 3.

The Author.

THERE is no prophet of whom less can be affirmed with certainty than Habakkuk. Not only do we know absolutely nothing about him personally, but dates as far apart as 701 and 330 B.C. have been proposed for him. This late date is based on subjective textual emendation and need not be considered here,[1] but the remaining uncertainty springs directly from the book itself.

The prophet begins (1: 2ff) by complaining about the iniquity and oppression around him. Though it is not stated who the oppressor is, the most natural interpretation is that the prophet is complaining about internal troubles, about the social wrongdoing so often condemned by the prophets. God answers (1: 5–11) by saying that He is doing something which none could anticipate or believe (ver. 5) in that He is on the point of raising up the Chaldeans (ver. 6; this is the force of the Hebrew), who will be God's instruments of punishment.

The prophet then remonstrates with God (1: 12–17), asking how He in His purity can use impure instruments, especially when they are as bad as those they are to punish (cf. 1: 13 with 1: 3f). After some delay (2: 1) God answers him, that in due course it will be seen that "the righteous shall live by his

---

[1] See Young, p. 263; Rowley: *The Growth of the Old Testament,* p. 117.

faithfulness," but those that are puffed up will perish (2: 2–5). The fate of the Chaldeans is then depicted in five woes (2: 6–20).

In Habakkuk's description of the behaviour of the Chaldeans there is no suggestion that we have to do with prophetic vision; it bears the stamp of being based on what he had heard of them, or even of what he had seen personally. As a result 1: 12–17 and 2: 6–20 can hardly be earlier than 612 B.C., the year of Nineveh's fall, and they may be even later than 605 B.C., when Nebuchadnezzar defeated Pharaoh Necho at Carchemish. In contrast 1: 5–11 can be given its obvious meaning only if it is dated at the latest shortly after 626 B.C., when Babylon recovered its independence under Nabopolassar the Chaldean.

If we leave to one side suggestions that have met with little approval, we find that scholars are divided between four different solutions of the difficulty:[1]

(1) 1: 5–11 are not really a prediction, but "the prophet throws himself dramatically into the past."[2]

(2) 1: 5–11 should be placed before 1: 2; they are the oldest part of the book and are possibly quoted by Habakkuk from an earlier prophet. Then 1: 2ff and 1: 12–17 form a continuous passage of complaint against the Chaldeans, there being no mention of unrighteous Israelites.

(3) 1: 5–11 should be placed after 2: 4. Then 1: 2ff represents a complaint against the oppression of Judah by the Assyrians, or perhaps the Egyptians; the prophet appeals to Jehovah (1: 12–17); Jehovah promises deliverance (2: 1–4) through the Chaldeans (1: 5–11), then follow five woes against the oppressor, whether Assyrians or Egyptians. (It is on the basis of this view that a date as early as 701 B.C. had been suggested for the prophecy.)

(4) The simplest explanation, though not entirely free of difficulty, is to refuse to see a normal prophecy in Habakkuk. It is a record not of Habakkuk's messages to the people but of his problems and God's answers. We are not suggesting that he did not prophesy, but that here we have an account of the inner conflict behind his public utterances. If it is so, we may assume the passage of a considerable period of time between 1: 5–11 and 1: 12–17. In this case the book may well extend over a period from at least 626 to 605 B.C. This view is the basis of the following notes.

Habakkuk's Message.

Habakkuk's contribution to our knowledge of God is found mainly in two passages.

[1] See HDB, article Habakkuk; ISBE, article Habakkuk.
[2] Lanchester: Nahum, Habakkuk and Zephaniah (C.B.) *ad loc.*

(1) Isaiah could explain the triumph of the Assyrian by his being the instrument of God's punishing (Isa. 10: 5f) who should be punished himself, when his work was done (Isa 10: 12). But Habakkuk (1: 13) cannot understand how a pure God can use impure instruments. It is to be noted that he receives no answer to his question. Faith can say as in Ps. 76: 10:

"Surely the wrath of man shall praise thee:
The residue of wrath shalt thou gird upon thee" (as an ornament)

but this is faith. The intellect is faced with moral problems in the Divine government of the universe to which it can find no full solution (see also note on Isa. 45: 7, p. 60).

(2) The centre of the prophecy is obviously the short message (2: 4) to be written so plainly (2: 2) "one may read it at a glance" (Moffatt):

"Behold, his soul is puffed up, it is not upright in him,
But the righteous shall live in his faithfulness (to Jehovah)."

The versions confirm by their variations the impression created by the English translation that the first line has been textually corrupted. Though we cannot now reconstruct it with certainty, its main thought is quite clear from the context.

Young's *Analytical Concordance* shows only two examples of the use of "faith" in the Old Testament, Hab. 2: 4 being one. In each case the correct translation is faithfulness. The Hebrew in his concrete thinking did not speak of faith, but of faithfulness toward God, and this in turn implied faith, *i.e.* trust—where faith in God does not lead to faithfulness, it is vain. The promise through Habakkuk is that the man who shows his trust in God by his faithfulness to God will find God faithful in keeping him.

Woe to the Oppressor (2: 6–20).

These five woes are a taunt-song (ver. 6; cf. Isa. 14: 4 and p. 51) taken up by the nations against the Chaldeans, though it should be obvious that the last is suitable only if spoken by the prophet himself. As in Amos 1: 3–2: 3 the woes are pronounced against acts that contravene man's sense of the fitness of things.

(1) ver. 6ff condemn the lust of conquest, which sheds blood for the sheer love of conquering.

(2) ver. 9ff take up the rapacity of the Chaldeans.

(3) ver. 12ff develop the previous woe. The squeezing of the conquered peoples was particularly for the rebuilding of

Babylon, which Nebuchadnezzar transformed into one of the wonders of the ancient world (cf. Dan. 4: 30).

(4) ver. 15ff condemn the wanton humiliation of the conquered; the picture of making them drunk is probably metaphorical. Ps. 137: 3 may refer to these wanton insults and cf. Dan. 5: 2.

(5) ver. 18ff—here it is the prophet that mocks Chaldean idolatry. Nebuchadnezzar was a very devout man. It is part of God's irony that Babylon fell to Cyrus partially at least through the treachery of the priests of Merodach.

God Comes to Deliver (Ch. 3).

This chapter is a psalm, which, if the musical rubrics are any guide, was probably taken from some temple collection of psalms. Its addition to the preceding chapters may well be due to an editor who wished to bring together all the extant work of Habakkuk. While we do not think that the psalm has any direct connexion with the preceding prophecy, we see in that a proof rather than the reverse of Habakkuk's authorship. The arguments for a post-exilic date for the psalm seem to be mainly subjective.

As Habakkuk prays for God's intervention in the turmoil around[1] he has a vision of Him coming as He once did at the Red Sea, Sinai, Jordan and in the Conquest; vers. 3–15 are based on the language of Deut. 33: 2; Judges 5: 4f; Ps. 68: 7f. While it is an account of what happened in the past, it is a present reality for the prophet. So we should read present tenses throughout from ver. 3 to ver. 15 as in the R.V. mg.

Though the first effect of the vision on the prophet is inner distress (ver. 16), it then creates in him the confident ability to endure even worse conditions than those he is passing through (ver. 17ff).

[1] Turmoil, rather than wrath—so G. A. Smith II, p. 150.

CHAPTER XI

JEREMIAH

THE STRUCTURE OF JEREMIAH

A. **Chs. 1-25: 14. Prophecies of Doom.**
  1—Ch. 1. The call of Jeremiah.
  2—Chs. 2-6. Prophecies from the time of Josiah.
  3—Chs. 7-20. Prophecies from the time of Jehoiakim.
  4—Chs. 21-25: 14. Prophecies against kings and prophets.
B. **Chs. 25: 15-38; 46-51. Prophecies against the Nations.***
C. **Chs. 26-33. Destruction and Restoration.**
D. **Chs. 34-45. Jeremiah and the last days of Jerusalem.**
E. **Ch. 52. An historical Appendix.**

* The order in the LXX irresistibly suggests that this was the original position of chapters 46-51. They are shown thus to bring out the similarity in structure between the first three sections of Jeremiah and "Proto-Isaiah" and Ezekiel.

The Neglected Prophet.

IF the length of a prophet's writings were any criterion of the number of books that should be written about him, then Jeremiah would be the most neglected of all the prophets. Though scholars are now beginning to atone for past neglect, it still persists in the pulpit and Bible class. For this there are at least three strong reasons.

Though most of the prophets employ poetry, and "Deutero-Isaiah" shows more sustained poetic structure, Jeremiah is the greatest lyric poet of them all. Only Hosea is comparable with him. With many of them we feel that they are merely using poetic forms, but Jeremiah is a poet. It need hardly be stressed that great poetry often demands much closer study than does prose to extract its full meaning.

There was always a tendency for the prophet's life to become part of his message, but with the exception of Jonah this is nowhere so marked as in Jeremiah. Indeed, toward the end of his work his life to a large extent became his message. Where it has not been grasped that Jeremiah's life is in itself a revelation of God, both his life and his spoken message have been seen out of focus.

The present form of the book is peculiar, and demands more preliminary study than is normally the case, if the true background and flow of events are to be accurately grasped.

The many striking differences between the Hebrew text and the LXX afford grounds for thinking that Baruch, indubitably the book's chief editor, may have died, perhaps by violence, before he had completed his task.

The Compiling of the Book.

A careful study of Jeremiah in English will probably reveal to most what is obvious in Hebrew, *viz.* that the contents may be divided into three groups: (i) Prophecies by Jeremiah in poetry; (ii) Prophecies by Jeremiah in prose; (iii) Stories about Jeremiah in prose.

The third is found mainly in chs. 34–45 (see structure of book), but is to be found also in chs. 1–25: 14 and chs. 26–33. There is no reasonable doubt that it is the work of Baruch, Jeremiah's companion and scribe (36: 4, etc.; 32: 12; 43: 3, 6; 45).

The second is found mainly in chs. 1–25: 14 but also in chs. 26–33. If compared carefully with the poetical prophecies, it gives the impression of being a report of Jeremiah's message rather than his actual words. Since it resembles the third group in style, it is reasonable to suppose that Baruch was responsible for these prose reports as well. Jeremiah's entirely undeserved reputation for prosiness is derived from these reports; prosiness is anyway relative and subjective. The fact that we have to do with an eye-witness condensation of some of Jeremiah's prophecies in no way affects their accuracy.

Ch. 36 tells us how the book began. It is impossible to know, and fruitless to guess, by how much the second roll (36: 32) was longer than the first (36: 2–4), but it is reasonable to suppose that it will have included the bulk of the poetical passages in the first two sections of the book and some of those in the third (see structure of book).

Later, perhaps in Egypt, Baruch will have woven his prose collection of Jeremiah's prophecies into this enlarged roll. He added also a few of the narrative stories he had written down about Jeremiah's sufferings.

It must be left an open question whether Baruch ever intended adding section D (chs. 34–45). It may well be that his friends were responsible for doing it after his death. This would help to explain the chronologically rather disjointed picture we have of Jeremiah. The historical chapters in the earlier sections of the book owe their present position to spiritual rather than chronological motives. Ch. 52 is a later historical appendix taken from II Kings—note 51: 64b.

Jeremiah the Young Man.

The peculiar importance of Jeremiah's life makes it advisable to use it as a framework within which to study the book as a whole. It so happens that the three kings under whom he prophesied, Josiah, Jehoiakim, and Zedekiah, coincide with the first three of the four periods of his prophetic activity.

Jeremiah was born of a priestly family (1: 1) in Anathoth, the modern Anata, a village about four miles to the north-east of Jerusalem, in the tribal portion of Benjamin.[1] The usual assumption is that he was a descendant of Abiathar (I Kings 2: 26). The banishment of his great ancestor did not necessarily imply that his descendants were barred from temple service in Jerusalem, and Hilkiah, his father, may well have officiated there as a priest. In any case, however, he was not Josiah's high priest (II Kings 22: 4)—the similarity in names will be accidental. The frequent suggestion that Jeremiah's father was priest of the village high place that will have been abolished by Josiah has little to commend it. Abiathar would not have been willing to serve at a village sanctuary, while a major sanctuary would not have been possible at that short distance from Jerusalem, nor would the expelled high priest have been allowed to found one.

Jeremiah never acted as priest, nor is there any evidence that he would have done so, had he not been called to be a prophet. The contrast between him and Ezekiel in this respect is remarkable (see ch. XIII).

Jeremiah will have been born about the year 645 B.C. toward the end of the reign of the evil king Manasseh. The way in which Jeremiah was steeped in the prophecies of his predecessors, especially Hosea, suggests that his home may have been one of those where the light of the persecuted prophetic tradition was kept alive in a dark age. The story of his call (ch. 1) suggests that he had been expecting it. His only protest was that he was too young (1: 6). On general grounds we may suppose him to have been between 18 and 20 at the time. The Hebrew word (na'ar) should not have been translated "child"; it means one who has not yet a recognized place in the community; while used of children, it refers more commonly to young unmarried men and to slaves.

His call came in 626 B.C. (1: 2). If we compare Chron. with Kings, we see that Josiah's reformation began in the year before (II Chron. 34: 3), though it did not reach its height and become effective till 621 B.C. (II Kings 22: 3; II Chron. 34: 8). From the human standpoint, this will have been the impulse that finally prepared Jeremiah for his call.

In spite of frequent assertions to the contrary, there is no real evidence that Jeremiah helped in Josiah's reformation, and very little, if any, that he really sympathized with it. It is

[1] For an excellent description of the surroundings see G. A. Smith: Jeremiah, pp. 67–72.

true that his earliest prophecies are directed mainly against the idolatry that the reformation was to sweep away for the time being (2: 1–3: 5; 3: 19–4: 4; note that 3: 19 is the immediate sequel of 3: 5), but in a prophecy probably only a little later (3: 6–13) he recognizes that the reformation is merely outward and feigned (3: 10). That is why his remaining prophecies from the time of Josiah give a picture of unrelieved gloom.

In modern text-books 11: 1–8 are generally referred to Jeremiah's activity during the time of the reformation. 11: 3f do not fit in with the insistence of the modern scholar that the book found (II Kings 22: 8) was Deuteronomy, for Jeremiah is obviously referring to the covenant at Sinai, not to something done at the end of the wilderness journey. The natural interpretation of ch. 11 would place it in the reign of Jehoiakim for the whole section seems to belong to his reign, the prophecies under Josiah ending with ch. 6. Still more important is it that 11: 1–14 is one of those prose reports of Jeremiah's sayings we have attributed with a high degree of probability to Baruch. There is no evidence, however, that Baruch was in touch with Jeremiah before the reign of Jehoiakim. It seems rather that once Jeremiah had convinced himself from the lack of changed lives (ch. 5) that the reformation was purely external, he dropped into the background, not wishing to embarrass a king he respected so highly (II Chron. 35: 25; Jer. 22: 15f). This would explain the lack of prophecies which can reasonably be attributed to the later years of Josiah.

It is instructive to note even in his early prophecy that deep sympathy and feeling that marks out Jeremiah, *e.g.* 4: 10, 19, and his feeling for nature, so rare in the Old Testament, *e.g.* 1: 11ff; 4: 25.

Jeremiah's Call (Ch. 1).

We have already referred to the call itself, but the accompanying "visions" need closer attention. We use the inverted commas because it is virtually certain that God spoke to him through two things he will have seen many a time before.

His eye fell on a branch of *waker* (*i.e.* almond), which had already awakened to the first breath of the coming spring and burst into blossom although the other trees seemed still wrapped in their winter sleep. Then the voice of God told him that even so the purposes of God were on the verge of waking into fulfilment, for He was waking over them (see R.V. mg. for word-play). Much that follows in Jeremiah is only understandable as we grasp that he was dominated by the knowledge that the judgment of God would break forth in his own day.

Then as he looked at the clouds, they seemed to take the

form of a huge, boiling cauldron leaning over from the north, ready to discharge its contents over Judah and Jerusalem. The stress does not lie primarily on the north, for the geography of Palestine demanded that invasion must come from the north, unless, indeed, it came from Egypt. Rather it is the supplementing of the former message by its stress that the instruments of God's doom were even then being prepared to be poured out as the hot anger of God over the land.

The Northern Invader (4: 5–31; 5: 15–19; 6: 1–8, 22–26).

This vivid prophetic portrayal of the fulfilment of 1: 13ff was probably lived through by Jeremiah in visions—see his personal anguish, 4: 19ff. Some have seen in them the Chaldeans, but for a long time the prevalent view has been that we have here the Scythians portrayed. We know that they shared in the convulsions that preceded the destruction of Nineveh in 612 B.C., but the Greek historian Herodotus is our only authority for the story that they swept down to the very frontier of Egypt, where the Pharaoh was glad to buy them off. Herodotus' account is, however, so vague and contains such demonstrable errors that it is probably best to ignore him. In any case some of the language is quite unsuited to the Scythians, so that those who hold this view have to assume that Jeremiah later worked over these poems adapting them to the Chaldeans. It is neither Scythian nor Chaldean that Jeremiah sees here. Just as 1: 13ff was silent as to what people should pour out of the cauldron of God's wrath, so here, when Jeremiah sees them, they are still unidentified. It is the sureness and terror of the doom that God reveals to His servant, not the identity of His executioners; that was to come later.

There is a progression in these visions. In 4: 5f the people are called to flee to the fenced cities, and especially to Jerusalem. The standard set up (ver. 6) is to act as a guide. But in 6: 1 the Benjamites are called on to flee from Jerusalem, to which they had previously fled for safety.

The reason for the change in attitude is caused by the prophet's realization of the moral corruption of Jerusalem (ch. 5). When it is grasped that this chapter must almost certainly be attributed to a time after 621 B.C., when Josiah's reform reached its height—note the lack of mention of idolatry in contrast to chs. 2 and 3, which are before the carrying through of the reform—we can begin to understand how superficial it had all been.

Faithless Israel (2: 1–4: 4).

In this section we have a number of short, passionate, poetic pleadings with Israel, forming a spiritual whole. Israel

F

throughout means both the Northern Kingdom, and Judah. Here, as elsewhere when he pleads with the Northern tribes, it is not clear whether Jeremiah is addressing himself to those in exile or to those who had been left behind in their land now ruled for Assyria by the Samaritan settlers.

This dual meaning of Israel has, however, been obscured by the insertion between 3: 5 and ver. 19 of an independent prophecy (3: 6–13) of slightly later date (see above) in which Israel is used exclusively of the Northern Kingdom in contrast to Judah. Its sense has been obscured by a wrong use of tense in the English versions. In 3: 6 we should have the past instead of the perfect tense, *i.e.* "Hast thou seen what backsliding Israel did? She went up . . . and there played the harlot." Jeremiah is referring to the closing days of the Northern Kingdom.

Ch. 3: 14–18 is an even later prophecy, perhaps from the time of Zedekiah, which is here inserted because of its spiritual suitability. The very important reference to the ark (3: 16) is dealt with below together with the passages in which Jeremiah gives his attitude toward ceremonial religion in general (see *The Vanity of Outward Religion*).

For the correct understanding of this section it must be borne in mind that Jeremiah is referring to two apparently distinct things, which yet for the prophet are indistinguishable. Obviously the sin above all others that is being condemned is idolatry, but equally obviously much of it was not seen in that light by the people—note especially 2: 23, where the charge of idolatry is definitely denied.

It would seem clear that from the time of the Judges on, checked by the good kings but not stamped out, the bulk of the people worshipped Jehovah in much the same way as they had seen the Canaanites worshipping their gods, the Baalim. In other words, they looked on Jehovah simply as their Baal. For the prophets, this was equivalent to worshipping Baal himself; they denied that it was Jehovah-worship at all. Along with this Baalized Jehovah-worship there was, of course, much worship of other gods as well. The important point is that unless we worship God as He wishes to be worshipped, He does not accept our worship at all. It is equivalent to the worship of other gods (see ch. V, p. 36ff.).

When Jeremiah convinces Israel of her sin, she merely says defiantly, "No hope; no! for I have loved strangers, and after them will I go" (2: 25).

Increasing Obduracy (6: 9–21).

It is likely there is a minor textual corruption in ver. 9; that in fact it is Jeremiah who is commanded to glean the remnant of Judah as a vine, to go over the people once again to see whether there is any who will accept the will of God.

Vers. 10–11a is Jeremiah's protest. Note how he identifies himself with God, so that the message of God's fury has become a burden within him longing to be poured out. Ver. 11b begins God's answer—not "I will pour it out" (A.V.), but "Pour it out" (R.V.).

Note that already Jeremiah is striking the note we are to hear so frequently later, and is condemning the false prophets, cf. 4: 10 (referring to the false message of assurance from the false prophets); 5: 31; 6: 13.

For 6: 20 see below *The Vanity of Outward Religion*.

The prophecies under Josiah end with a word of encouragement; in spite of apparent failure he had been doing the task allotted him. The people are compared with base metal (6: 28–30).

Chs. 1–6 of Jeremiah underline the need of reading the prophetic books along with the histories of the kings in Kings and Chronicles. Without them we are bound to get a one-sided view. In Kings and Chronicles Josiah's reformation seems to be a complete success, and it is difficult to understand the collapse after his death. From Jeremiah we see that it was but the last effort to shore up the doomed and collapsing house of Judah, and there was never any hope of success. It only, by delaying the final catastrophe, made it the greater when it came.

Jeremiah and the Reign of Jehoiakim.

The long list of chapters[1] in the footnote is only approximately correct. Shorter portions in 7–20 and 46–49: 33 may be from the time of Zedekiah, while portions of 30, 31 may well be from that of Jehoiakim. But these minor doubts cannot obscure the fact that the major part of Jeremiah's prophetic activity took place at this time. If what we have written above is at all correct, Jeremiah did not come prominently into the public eye so long as Josiah lived. No sooner had Jehoiakim settled himself firmly on the throne than Jeremiah stepped into the limelight and stayed there, the best-hated man in the kingdom. We cannot understand what happened without a study of the historical background.

The Historical Background.

The fulfilment of Isaiah's prophecies at the time of Sennacherib's invasion seems to have created a fanatical belief in the inviolability of Jerusalem; and there is every evidence that this was heightened by the reform of religion under Josiah. Huldah's prophecy (II Kings 22: 18–20) was doubtless subject to the general principle of Jer. 18: 7–10 (cf. ch. I), but as Judah's prosperity increased under wise rule, this will have

[1] Chs. 7–20; 22: 1–19; 23: 9–40; 25, 26; 35, 36; 46–49: 33.

become increasingly forgotten, and the threat of divine punishment (II Kings 22: 16f) will have faded away into the distant future; Isaiah's message of the remnant (see p. 49) had not been learnt.

When Nineveh fell in 612 B.C., the popular mind must have visualized the return of former glories. Only in this way can we explain Josiah's armed opposition to Pharaoh Necho's expedition in 609 (II Kings 23: 29). It was the height of madness, but we may be sure that the professional prophets of Jerusalem were as unanimous in favour of the king's action as Ahab's were, when he went up to Ramoth Gilead and perished (I Kings 22: 6).

It is probably impossible for us to realize how great a shock Josiah's death must have been to all but a handful of his subjects. The greater must have been the relief and the wonder when a few months later they found that Necho demanded no more than a king of his choice, Eliakim or Jehoiakim (II Kings 23: 34), and a heavy tribute. Once again the House of Jehovah had guaranteed the inviolability of Jerusalem.

The Challenge (Ch. 7: 1–15; 26: 1–19, 24).

Jeremiah, who had been repelled by the outwardness of Josiah's reformation, saw the position and its dangers so clearly that he decided that the people must face the truth at once. At the first suitable moment (26: 1) he announced in the entry of the court of the temple (7: 2; 26: 2) that unless there was a *moral* reformation the temple would be destroyed as was the sanctuary in Shiloh (presumably after Eli's death, I Sam, 4: 18), and the people would go into exile.

Ch. 7: 1–15 is a summary of his message, while 26: 1–19, though including the message, is mainly concerned with the' results. For the people, Jeremiah's action was unpardonable, for he was undermining their chief confidence; in addition, there is nothing more dangerous than to attack popular religion. It hardly needs saying that they found natural leaders in the priests and sanctuary prophets (26: 7). When brought to trial before the princes, Jeremiah found men who probably had little love for the priests, and so received a fair trial. The evidence that saved him (26: 17ff) was the evidence of similar prophesying by Micaiah, *i.e.* Micah (3: 12). Though the evidence follows the verdict (26: 16) by a common artifice in Hebrew story-telling, it should be clear that it was in fact the cause of the verdict. The fickle crowd sided for the time being with the judges, but 26: 24 strongly suggests that the priests, secure in their knowledge of the royal attitude (26: 20–23), stirred up the people to lynch Jeremiah, and were only foiled by Ahikam; or did they appeal to the king?

In the English versions 26: 20–23 is printed as though it were part of the elders' evidence. This is manifestly false. It is doubtful whether, on chronological ground, we could even date it before Jeremiah's challenge. It is inserted to show the royal attitude to troublesome prophets, and the danger that Jeremiah ran by his bold challenge.

The Vanity of Outward Religion.[1]

An immediate result of Jehoiakim's accession was the rapid re-introduction of the evil practices that Josiah had cleared away. We find fewer mentions of idolatry than earlier in 2: 1–4: 4, for God made it clear to Jeremiah that the re-introduction of idolatry was the beginning of a no-longer-postponable end (7: 16–20) so there was little point in rebuking it. This thought that the renewed idolatry had put them beyond the power of intercessory prayer is repeated in 11: 9–14 and 14: 10–12 (cf. also in a slightly different context 15: 1).

Even worse for Jeremiah was the re-introduction into Jehovah worship of the abominations of heathenism. 7: 31 makes it clear that the children were offered to Jehovah (". . . which I commanded not, neither came it into my mind"), cf. also 19: 3–9. In 8: 7 Jeremiah uses a remarkable picture from nature to illustrate the unnatural conduct of Judah; it reminds us of Isaiah 1: 3, but is stronger.

It would seem, however, that in these early years of Jehoiakim's reign, Jeremiah's main concern was with the subtly false rather than the grossly false in religion. No prophet goes further in his rejection of all outward religion, but, in order to obtain a balanced interpretation we must not forget that Jeremiah knew for certain that the temple and all its ceremonial were doomed to destruction in a few years' time.

His most striking utterance on sacrifices is in 7: 21–26. He begins by mockingly calling on his hearers to break the fundamental laws of sacrifice (ver. 21). The "sacrifices" are the peace offerings, which were in large measure eaten by the worshippers; Jeremiah tells them to treat the burnt-offerings, where not even the sacrificing priest had a share (Lev. 1; 6: 8–11), in exactly the same way—Jehovah did not care. He had not put details of sacrifices first when He made known His will after the Exodus. In the fundamental covenant (Exod. 20–23) the Decalogue takes pride of place, and details of sacrificial ritual have only a few passing references, mainly the prohibition of certain Canaanite practices.

[In older critical works, this verse is used as a proof that the Priestly Code is post-exilic, but since the Ras Shamra excavations the argument has been dropped. The English

[1] 3: 16; 6: 20; 7: 21–26; 8: 8f; 9: 25f; 11: 1–8; 14: 10–12.

"concerning burnt-offerings" is too weak; the Hebrew should be translated "concerning details of . . .," cf. A.V. mg.]

The same thought is taken up in 11: 1–8. The popular concept was that the fundamental part of the covenant was sacrifice. Jeremiah insists that it is obedience (cf. I Sam. 15: 22).

In 14: 12 the formal fast is rejected and in 9: 25f the physical fact of circumcision. This passage points to the little-known fact that circumcision was not confined to Israel, or even to descendants of Abraham.[1] The R.V. should be consulted here. "Circumcised in their uncircumcision" (R.V.) means there is no circumcised heart to match the circumcised body.

Jeremiah goes further still. In 3: 16 (probably from the reign of Zedekiah) he says that the vanished Ark will neither be missed nor made again (R.V. mg.), because that which it symbolized, the Throne of Jehovah (ver. 17), will have become a reality in Jerusalem. He thus enunciates the principle that all outward helps to religion have purely a symbolic, not an objective, value.

Even the written Scriptures come under his condemnation (8: 8f, see R.V.). The scribes and the wise men were rejecting the prophetic message ("the word of Jehovah" ver. 9) by appealing to the written Law of the Lord. But wherever blind or perverse interpretation of Scripture makes the reader insensible to the Word of the Lord, then the Scriptures have become a falsehood. They need the inner power of the Spirit for their right use as much as any other physical aspect of religion, otherwise they will only lead astray.

That Jeremiah was not objecting to the externals of religion as such may be seen by his commendation of Sabbath observance (as a proof of obedience!) in 17: 19–27, and his clear emphasis that there would be sacrifices after the restoration (17: 26; 31: 14; 33: 18).

Increasing Opposition.

It is abundantly clear that Jeremiah was never forgiven his outspoken words in the temple. One sign of his increasing unpopularity is his use of symbolic actions intended to catch the eye of those whose ears were closed.

The first example is given in 13: 1–11, where the story of Jeremiah's fine linen girdle is told. There is, however, a strong possibility that it was a visionary action. The round trip would be some 800 miles, and the story demands that he

---

[1] For details see article Circumcision in HDB and ISBE. The excavations at Ras Shamra have shown that it was also a Canaanite custom. It was the Philistine who in and near Palestine was uncircumcised.

should have made it twice. If so, how obdurate had the people become! A less likely explanation is that he used a stream north of Anathoth with a similar name. In 13: 12–14 we find him gaining a hearing by the use of dark sayings. But the people were to be yet more hardened. As often, catastrophe (drought, 14: 1–6) turned people away from God rather than to Him. And so Jeremiah was told that *he* was to be his message; he was not to marry (16: 2); he was not to enter the house of mourning (16: 5), nor was he to share in the joy of the marriage feast (16: 8). Even if we make full allowance for lack of chronological order, we are compelled to accept that we are now drawing near to the end of Jeremiah's regular public utterances.

One last warning he would give. He collected leading personalities (19: 1) and carrying a jar (a woman's work!) he went at their head to the Valley of Hinnom through the streets of Jerusalem. The story leaves us to imagine the huge crowd that will have rapidly formed and followed. The solemn breaking of the jar (19: 10) spoke its message to those who stopped their ears to the message of doom. Further symbolic actions are recorded in chs. 35, 27 (note ver. 1 should read "In the beginning of the reign of Zedekiah," cf. ver. 3), 32, 43: 8–13.

Rejection.

Jeremiah had to share the experience of so many that "a man's foes shall be they of his own household" (Matt. 10: 36). One of his most shattering experiences was to find that his own family (12: 6) was treacherously plotting his murder (11: 18–12: 6). The reason was injured family pride (11: 21). Ever since his address in the temple he was a marked man, and his aristocratic family resented sharing in his notoriety.

A couple of years later (18: 19–23) Jeremiah discovered a more widespread plot to kill him. The motives are not indicated, but they can easily be guessed.

After his solemn message of doom by the breaking of the jar (see above) Jeremiah repeated the gist of his message in the temple (19: 14f). Pashhur, the priest responsible for order within the sacred precincts (20: 1) arrested him, put him in the stocks and left him there all night (20: 2f). The failure of any to intervene must have been the final proof to Jeremiah of his friendlessness. Whether the smiting was a flogging or just a blow it was a supreme indignity for a man of aristocratic family, for whom death was better than a blow.

In the fourth year of Jehoiakim (25: 1; 36: 1—605 B.C.), Nebuchadnezzar defeated Necho at Carchemish, and at one stroke became lord of the lands as far as the Egyptian frontier. Jehoiakim had to bow to a new lord (Dan. 1: 1; for the date see p. 142). God told Jeremiah to make one last appeal. Baruch, Jeremiah's friend and scribe (36: 4) took down a summary of Jeremiah's messages up to date, and awaited an opportunity to read them to the people. Jeremiah was restrained (36: 5, R.V., mg.) from entering the temple, presumably as a sequel to 20: 1–6. A fast day the following year gave the desired opportunity (obviously ver. 8 anticipates ver. 9).

What the result with the people might have been, we cannot say, for the curiosity of the high officials of state caused them to intervene and they brought the matter before the king, who will have already been ill-disposed to the prophet, thanks to the biting condemnation of 22: 13–19. He dismissed the whole message of the roll contemptuously and would have arrested and executed Jeremiah. He and Baruch had to go underground, and it was probably only as the shadow of Nebuchadnezzar fell across the city, that Jeremiah could emerge again, vindicated as a prophet indeed (35: 1, 11).

Jeremiah and the False Prophets.

It would be unfair to assume that the majority of the false prophets were deliberate deceivers, at least at first. But the moment the prophet became a professional, attached to a sanctuary, his bread and butter depended on his not offending unduly against popular opinion, and above all on his getting results. No delay like that of Jeremiah's (42: 7) would ever have been tolerated from a professional. How great the temptation could be, may be judged by the fact that Jeremiah must have been intellectually certain all through the critical time of waiting what God's word would finally be.

Just because the professional prophets were not mere deceivers, because adulterated truth is so hard to distinguish from unadulterated, because spirituality is so easily imitated, because book knowledge can so easily replace inspiration, the distinguishing of true from false prophets was never easy. One thing was clear to all: God would not speak with two different voices. The religious world is always tempted to be on the side of the big battalions, so when Jeremiah stood alone faced by the other prophets, he found the people against him, denouncing him as a deceiver or madman; at times he was tempted to doubt himself. He did not have that overpowering, monumental character that seems to have made Isaiah almost impervious to opposition.

Why Hilkiah inquired of Huldah about the book of the law is not clear (II Kings 22: 14); certainly Josiah had his professional prophets (II Kings 23: 2). Perhaps the high priest knew them too well. Probably it was their reiterated prophecies of prosperity that first awoke Jeremiah to the problem involved (4: 10). He was soon to realize the amount of evil among the prophets (5: 30f), who were willing to sell themselves for money (6: 13).

As Jeremiah was increasingly rejected in the early years of Jehoiakim, he found the burden of standing out alone against the prophets growing ever greater (14: 13–18). Through it he learnt to understand the nature of true prophecy better. We may reasonably attribute the collection of prophecies against the false prophets to this period (23: 9–40). The opening passage stresses the terrible consequences, when the prophet plays false. The remainder shows how deeply Jeremiah had been led to understand the true nature of prophecy, an understanding of real importance for to-day.

A prophetic dream was no guarantee of truth, for the dream might be the expression of the prophet's own desires (vers. 16, 25ff), or his unconscious, to use the language of modern psychology. Equally the fact that the message might be true was no guarantee that the bearer had been entrusted with it; he might be simply borrowing from another (ver. 30). There were two signs of the true prophet: an outward—if his message were accepted, it would transform lives (ver. 22); and an inward—the prophet's knowledge that he had stood in God's council chamber (vers. 18, 22).

The Moulding of the Prophet.

The dual pressure of rejection and of having to face the implications of his prophetic calling led to a spiritual development that can best be compared with that of Job's. The passages that picture it should be closely studied, viz. 8: 18–9: 2; 10: 23ff; 11: 18–12: 6; 15: 10–21; 18: 18–23; 20: 7–18.

Since chs. 1–20 represent approximately the enlarged roll (36: 32, see p. 78), we must assume that both the insertion of these personal passages, and their position in the prophecy, are the work of Jeremiah himself. When we realize that 20: 7–18 is the end and climax of the roll, we also realize that these passages are essential to an understanding of Jeremiah's message.

His inner burden began with Jeremiah's inability to dissociate himself from those to whom he brought God's message of doom (8: 18—9: 2; and already 4: 19ff). This identification of himself with his people is seen in 10: 23ff, where the prayer is for them as well as for himself. Jeremiah's attitude foreshadows our Lord's on Olivet (Luke 19: 41–44).

Jeremiah's spiritual sufferings grew greater when his family tried to murder him (11: 18—12: 6). Quite apart from the enormity of their attempted action, which probably still lay within the power of the head of the family, the exclusion of a man from his family group was a blow worse than death itself, as may be seen from the violence of Jeremiah's reaction. The only consolation that God had for him was that much worse was to come (12: 5; the pride—A.V., swelling—of Jordan is the wild beast infested jungle that fringes the stream).[1]

Universal rejection and hatred broke Jeremiah down, and he turned to God in his fierce agony (15: 10–21; the LXX suggests strongly that the text of ver. 11 is corrupt, while there is no really satisfactory explanation for vers. 12–14). His agony carried him so far that he virtually blasphemed (ver. 18), almost comparing Jehovah to the broken cisterns he had equated the false gods with (2: 13). There is no sympathy apparent in God's answer; He shocked him to his senses by His call to conversion (ver. 19, if thou return, cf. Luke 22: 32), if he wished his prophetic ministry to continue.

The last straw for Jeremiah was his exclusion not merely from the society of his fellow-men (18: 18–23), but also from the temple (see above). He turned to God in even greater but fluctuating agony (20: 7–18). He accused God of deceiving or, better, enticing (mg.) him. The word stresses the simplicity of the one deceived; it is used in Exod. 22: 16 of the seducing of a girl. It is deliberately one of the ugliest words that he could have used. He accused God of having enticed him under false pretences into becoming a prophet, and then of having forced him to remain one. His cry to God ends with the wish that he had never been born (vers. 14–18, cf. Job 3).

So the curtain falls on the prophet, rejected by family and nation, his life in danger, excluded from the worship of the nation, and apparently cut off from his God. We do not know how God dealt with him in the years while he hid from Jehoiakim and the king's doom drew near; but before that doom fell, Jeremiah appeared again, fearless and unshakable. There is no evidence that he had come to understand the message of the Suffering Servant, and hence of his own sufferings; but he had learnt that it was as an individual that one had to come to God, and as an individual one had to be sustained by Him. In his spiritual agony we may see in Jeremiah a dim foreshadowing of our Lord.

Jeremiah and the Fall of Jerusalem.[2]

The promises of restoration (30–33) are a collection of short prophecies, most of which are earlier; some, however, will be from this period. Note that many of them deal especially

---

[1] For a description see G. A. Smith: *A Historical Geography of the Holy Land*, p. 483f; N. Glueck: *The River Jordan*, p. 63.

[2] *Chs.* 21; 22: 20–23: 8; 24; 27–34; 37–39; 49: 34–39; 50–51.

with the restoration of the North, *viz.* most of chs. 30, 31. The *approximate* order of the narrative sections is 24; 29; 27, 28; 21; 34: 1–7; 37: 3–10; 34: 8–22; 37: 11–21; 32, 33; 38: 1–28a; 39: 15–18; 38: 28b—39: 14.

It will be noted that apart from promises of restoration not many prophecies are attributed to Jeremiah. He had said all that needed saying, and the death of Jehoiakim and the exile of Jehoiachin had vindicated his message. All that was left for him was to rub in the grim moral as needed.

When the remnant in Jerusalem began to believe that the storm of judgment had passed them by because of their merits, they were told that on the contrary the exiles had been taken away to save them from the wrath to come (ch. 24, and cf. ch. XIII, p. 102). When false prophets promised the exiles a hope of speedy return, Jeremiah insisted that there was no hope until the fixed time of God's judgment had run its course (ch. 29).

Already when Nebuchadnezzar had scattered the army of Pharaoh Necho at Carchemish, Jeremiah had recognized in him and the Chaldeans the fulfilment of his earlier visions, and he had proclaimed him as the man of God's appointing against whom no one could stand (25: 9, 11). This conviction enabled him to stand against the attempts to form an anti-Babylonian conspiracy in the fourth year of Zedekiah (chs. 27, 28) and to deflect the weak king of Judah from it in spite of the assurances of the court prophets.

This conviction also explains his attitude during the final siege of Jerusalem. Zedekiah's rebellion was not only a breach of his oath (II Chron. 36: 13; Ezek. 17: 13–21), but also opposition to the ruler of God's choice. Submission was a sign of loyalty to Jehovah. No wonder that he was considered to be in the pay of the Chaldeans (37: 13; 38: 4).

A little-known incident is contained in 34: 8–22. Apparently when Nebuchadnezzar drew near Jerusalem, all Jewish slaves were freed. The motives were probably mixed, partly guilty conscience (ver. 13ff; Exod. 21: 2; Deut. 15: 12), partly the desire for extra fighters. With the withdrawal of the Chaldeans (37: 5, 11), the solemn covenant (ver. 18f) had been broken and the slaves enslaved once more. Jeremiah immediately showed the same burning zeal for social righteousness that marked out all the true prophets.

The New Covenant (31: 31–34).

Under Josiah Jeremiah evidently worked among the remnants of the northern tribes that were still in Palestine. After Necho's triumph this area was again detached from Judah, and Jeremiah could no longer visit them. So in the time he was hiding from Jehoiakim he will have written down his message of hope in chs. 30, 31.   After the fall of Jerusalem the collection, *The Book of Hope*, was enlarged to apply to the South as well.

The message of the new covenant could be proclaimed by him, because he had first experienced it himself.   It would not need either laws written in stone or teachers to instruct men in it.   Here was one who had been denounced by both priests and prophets, but though he had stood alone, he had yet been proved right.   In his heart God had written His will.

All prophecy is of necessity partial (Heb. 1: 1) and so Jeremiah did not rise to the whole truth.   God revealed to him that true religion cannot be external or bound to externals. What Jeremiah apparently did not grasp was the universalism we find in Isa. 19: 23ff, or at least not in this connexion.   The new covenant can no more be linked to national origin than to any other externals.   That a man is a physical descendant of Abraham means in itself nothing to God (Matt. 3: 9).   But the fact that when the new covenant was ratified at Golgotha by the blood of the Lamb of God it was freed from every national limitation, does not mean that we must dismiss the nationalistic setting of Jer. 31 as meaningless or spiritualize it into thin air. Rom. 11: 26 shows that it has a yet future application to all Israel.

It is one thing to say that Jeremiah was not given to see what the new covenant would mean for the world, it is entirely another to say that by Israel and Judah he really meant the Church.   So to understand Jer. 31: 23–40; 33: 14–26 is to make all sane Bible interpretation impossible.   On the other hand, we must not fall into the opposite error of supposing that the new covenant will mean something else for "all Israel" than it does for the Church, that saved Israel will be saved in some other way than is the Church.   God does not abolish physical Israel, but in saving it transcends it, just as He does not scrap this earth but renews it.

The Messiah (23: 5f; 30: 9, 21(?); 33: 14–26).

We refer to these Messianic passages not so much for their intrinsic importance as for the light they cast on prophetic interpretation generally.

There is little, if anything, in these passages that goes beyond the revelation given through earlier prophets.   But their occurrence shows that Jeremiah fully shared the Messianic hopes of his predecessors.   Why, then, do they play such a small part in his message, instead of being the focus of future hopes as in Isa. 1–35?   (The question presupposes not the prophet's free choice of message, but that the Spirit's message, in ways beyond our knowledge, shaped itself to the spiritual experience and understanding of the prophet.)

The most obvious reason is that it was the same motive as led Jeremiah to attack all externals in religion that distracted men from the inner truth. For the people the king was God's anointed, and therefore a pledge of His favour. Before the people could take comfort in the Righteous Branch, or Shoot (23: 5), they had to face the grim fact that the royal tree would have to be hewn down (36: 30; 22: 30; 39: 6; cf. Isa. 11: 1).

Relative silence in a book of the Bible on a matter already revealed does not imply either ignorance or dissent.

The Last Days of Jeremiah (Chs. 40–45).

When Jerusalem fell at last, Jeremiah received his supreme vindication by God. He was the one man from among the whole people who was left completely and absolutely at liberty (40: 4f).

With the world before him, there must have been a strong temptation to go to Babylonia, where he would have received a warm welcome from the better elements taken there with Jehoiachin. What a shelter for his old age one like Daniel would have made for him! On the other hand he might have sought a shelter somewhere in a less devastated corner of his own land. But Jeremiah was bound to his own people. He had served them in good and evil times for forty years, and now he stayed with those that needed him most (40: 6); but from them he was to experience the final mockery.

Asked by the leaders of the people what they should do after the murder of Gedaliah (42: 1–6), he spent ten days in prayer before he knew for certain that the insistent voice of heart and mind was also the voice of God (42: 7–18)—no other answer would have been consistent with his earlier prophecies; but that did not free him from the obligation of seeking God's face. Note that in accordance with frequent Hebrew practice, the whole of Jeremiah's answer is put together, though 42: 19–22 is obviously Jeremiah's answer after he had been accused of lying and acting as Baruch's tool (43: 3).

Though the people accused him of lying and rejected his message, yet they dragged him with them into Egypt (43: 6). Though they were unwilling to believe the prophet, they could not do without him. That is the tragedy of Judah—and of many a religious man. He could not do without God, but he would not obey Him; he constantly reformed, yet ever hankered after his old idolatry (ch. 44).

In Isaiah we have the Church foreshadowed in the remnant; in Jeremiah we have the Church made possible by the individual's living contact with the living God unbound by the ties of family, country or religion.

Jeremiah's Prophecies against the Nations (Chs. 46–51).

The bulk of these prophecies, chs. 46–49: 33—though 46: 13–28 may be later—come from the fourth year of Jehoiakim after the battle of Carchemish, or shortly after. As with the similar prophecies in Isaiah and Ezekiel their main purpose is to teach Israel, not the nations concerned. By stressing the extent of Nebuchadnezzar's power Jeremiah wants to teach Judah that God has given Judah to the Babylonian king as well. At the same time 27: 1–3, which depicts Jeremiah sending messages to the kings of the surrounding countries, makes it quite plausible that these oracles were sent to them too at a somewhat earlier date.

It seems impossible to justify the presence of the oracle against Damascus (49: 23–27), for Syria had lost its independent existence in the time of Isaiah. It has probably crept in from some earlier prophet. We do not know the reasons that motivated the somewhat later oracle against Elam (49: 34–39). That a prophecy against Babylon was not without personal risks to the prophet is shown by Jeremiah's use of two cyphers: *Sheshach* for Babylon (25: 26, 51: 41), and *Leb-qamai* for Chaldea (51: 1).

On the relationship of Jer. 49: 7–22 to Obad. 1–14 see ch. XII.

CHAPTER XII

OBADIAH

Obadiah and Jeremiah.

OUR interpretation of Obadiah must in measure depend on the date we give it, and this is turn depends on how we explain the connexion of vers. 1–9 with Jer. 49: 7–22. If we read the two side by side, it should be obvious that some connexion exists. The relevant parallelisms are:

Obad. vers. 1–4	Jer. 49: 14–16
vers. 5, 6	9, 10
vers. 8, 9a	7b, 22b

The connexion is explained in three main ways:—

(1) Jeremiah quoted from Obadiah. This, formerly the most widely held view, has a great deal to be said in its favour. The capture of Jerusalem described in ver. 11 would be that mentioned in II Chron. 21: 16f, *c.* 843 B.C. If this is so, Obadiah is the oldest of the prophetic books; this would explain its apparently primitive picture of the Day of the Lord, its early position in the Book of the Twelve, and indeed why it was preserved for us. Its position among The Twelve suggests that the Jewish scribes accepted that the evidence pointed to its use by Jeremiah.[1]

The arguments against this view are almost conclusive. If the Edomites had behaved in such a way as the prophecy suggests at the capture of the city in 843 B.C., it is very hard to understand why the writer of Chronicles did not mention them. Further, if the disaster to Jerusalem had been on the scale suggested by vers. 11–14, it is very strange that it was passed over in silence by Kings, while II Chron. 21: 16f makes the impression of little more than a plundering raid. No other capture of Jerusalem, except that by Nebuchadnezzar in 586 B.C. will fit the picture, for those mentioned in I Kings 14: 25f, II Kings 14: 8–14 are on various grounds unsuitable.

(2) Obadiah used Jer. 49: 7–22. Though this view has received little support, Aalders[2] seems to be correct, when he maintains that it is proved by the use of the feminine "her"

---

[1] See ISBE, article Obadiah, Book of; Young, p. 252f; Kirkpatrick, pp. 34–40.

[2] Aalders: *Recent Trends in Old Testament Criticism,* p. 15.

in Obad. ver. 1. Nowhere else, except Mal. 1: 4, is Edom feminine, and in this one exception the use is probably correctly explained by G. A. Smith, "The verb in the feminine indicates that the population of Edom is meant."[1] This cannot be applied to Obad. ver. 1. The parallel in Jer. 49: 14 also has the feminine, but it refers not to Edom but to Bozrah, which is feminine. So it would seem that Obadiah quoted this verse from Jeremiah without altering the grammar.

In spite of difficulties made or left unsolved by this view, it does make the capture of Jerusalem referred to in vers. 11–14 the capture by Nebuchadnezzar in 586 B.C., when as we know from Ezek. 35, Ps. 137: 7; Lam. 4: 21f, the Edomites did so behave. It should be noted too that in contrast to Obadiah, Jer. 49: 7–22, which is dated 605 B.C. (Jer. 46: 1f), brings no specific charge against Edom.

(3) The most commonly held view to-day is that both Obadiah and Jer. 49: 7–22 are quoting an older prophecy. That this is possible may be seen from the analagous cases of Isa. 2: 2–5; Mic. 4: 1–5 (see pp. 48, 63) and Isa. 15f (see p. 52). Since, however, this view normally assumes that Jer. 49: 7–22 is not by Jeremiah, does not answer Aalders' argument and is no more effective than the second view in meeting certain inherent difficulties in a late date for Obadiah, we are not attracted by it.[2] It agrees with the second view in making the capture of Jerusalem that in 586 B.C. We shall probably be safe in accepting that Obadiah cannot have been written before that date.

The Date of Obadiah.

Though we have decided that Obadiah will not be earlier than 586 B.C. we must still decide whether the verbs in vers. 2, 6f refer to the past, or whether they are prophetic perfects.

In the sixth century B.C. there seems to have been a wave of pressure by the Nabatean and other Arab tribes on the lands east of Jordan. By the time of Malachi, c. 450 B.C., Edom may well have already been driven from her old territory (Mal. 1: 3f). Already by the time of the return in 538 B.C. the South of Judaea as far as north of Hebron seems to have been in Edomite hands, and remained so until conquered and forcibly Judaized by John Hyrcanus, c. 125 B.C., thus opening the way for the half Edomite Herod to become king of the Jews. We know that Petra was in the hands of the Nabateans in 312 B.C., but they may have conquered it much earlier.

We shall probably be safe in assuming that the verbs in

[1] G. A. Smith II, p. 352.

[2] For an exposition of this view see HDB, article, Obadiah, Book of.

vers. 2, 6f are prophetic perfects, and that Obadiah prophesied early in the exile, when the Edomites were already moving into Judaean territory under Nabatean pressure, but before their traditional territory was seriously threatened. This would make Obadiah the only prophet prophesying on Judaean soil during the exile, and would go a long way towards explaining why this, by far the shortest of the prophets, was preserved. It would also explain why the sin of Judah is not mentioned in connexion with the Day of the Lord—for Judah in exile was already under Jehovah's judgment—and why special stress is laid on Israel possessing his possessions (ver. 17). A prophet's vision of the future is normally influenced by the circumstances of his own day.

The Coming Destruction of Edom (vers. 1–14, 15b).

It should be noticed that almost certainly the two halves of ver. 15 have been transposed, perhaps through an early scribal misunderstanding of ver. 16. "As thou hast done, it shall be done unto thee; thy dealing shall return upon thine own head" is the end of the judgment on Edom. The first half of the verse ushers in the second half of the prophecy.

We have a play upon words in ver. 7; for the R.V. text see II Sam. 3: 21 (send away), for the R.V. mg. see Exod 6: 1 (let go, *i.e.* drive out). The former is what one would expect from one's confederates; the latter is the grim reality.

The imperatives in ver. 12ff do not look to the future. Just as in the prophetic perfects of vers. 2, 6f the prophet is transported to the future and sees the doom already completed, so here he is transported into the past and speaks as though the Edomite hostility against Jerusalem had not yet taken place.

The Day of the Lord (vers. 15a, 16–21).

For the general concept of the Day of the Lord see ch. II. The drinking in ver. 16 is the drinking of the cup of God's wrath, of which Judah and Israel ("ye") have already drunk.

There is probably some textual corruption in ver. 19f, for as it stands it would seem to deprive the restored of Israel of part of their territory (both vers. 18 and 20 imply Israel's restoration); in ver. 20 quite apart from our ignorance of the location of Sepharad and why it should be specially mentioned, the Hebrew is very difficult.

Though Obadiah may seem preoccupied with the restoration of Israel, the closing words of the prophecy show that he knew that all this was to come to pass merely that the kingdom of God should be established.

CHAPTER XIII

EZEKIEL

THE STRUCTURE OF EZEKIEL

A. **Chs. 1-24. Prophecies of Doom.**
  1—Chs. 1-7. The Call and the opening message.
  2—Chs. 8-19. The Sin of Jerusalem.
  3—Chs. 20-23. The deeper meaning of the Sin.
  4—Ch. 24. Imminent Judgment.
B. **Chs. 25-32. Prophecies against the Nations.**
  1—Ch. 25. Palestine's Neighbours.
  2—Chs. 26-28. Tyre.
  3—Chs. 29-32. Egypt.
C. **Chs. 33-48. Prophecies of Restoration.**
  1—Ch. 33. The Prophet's function.
  2—Ch. 34. Rulers past and future.
  3—Chs. 35, 36. The Land.
  4—Ch. 37. The People.
  5—Chs. 38, 39. The last Enemies.
  6—Chs. 40-48. The Redeemed People at Peace.

THE problems connected with Ezekiel are of a very different kind from those dealt with in earlier chapters. There are no generally accepted problems of authorship, as in Isaiah. Still less does the book contain structural difficulties of the kind we find in Jeremiah. Ezekiel would seem to have put his book together himself, and he carefully dated the various sections, *viz.* 1: 2; 8: 1; 20: 1; 24: 1; 26: 1; 29: 1; 29: 17; 30: 20; 31: 1; 32: 1; 32: 17; 33: 21; 40: 1. In addition, for reasons to be considered later, we have no longer the short oracles linked often only by spiritual connexions we have become familiar with in the earlier prophets; for the most part the book consists of full-length addresses or writings. The problems relate rather to the prophet's personality and activities, and to the interpretation of some parts of his book.

Ezekiel's Early Life.

If our interpretation of 1: 1 is correct (see below), Ezekiel was born in 622 B.C. This means that he was over twenty years younger than Jeremiah, and that he was an infant in arms, when Josiah's reformation was sweeping the outward signs of idolatry out of Judah.

We have no information about his father, Buzi, beyond that he was of priestly family. The respect, however, accorded to Ezekiel by the elders of the people in exile (8: 1; 14: 1; 20: 1), and his being considered important enough to be taken into exile with Jehoiachin (cf. II Kings 24: 14) suggest that his was among the more important of the priestly families.

We are not told definitely in the Old Testament at what age the priest was to start his duties; there is no definite information on the subject in the Talmud with regard to New Testament times. There is, however, an intrinsic probability that it was thirty (cf Num. 4: 3, and perhaps Luke 3: 23, though this may link rather with II Sam. 5: 4). Since, however, a meticulous observance of every detail of the ritual was expected of the priest, a long period of preparation was normal for the young men of priestly family. It is quite clear from his prophecies that Ezekiel, unlike Jeremiah, had early steeped himself in the priestly traditions, and had learnt all the details of his holy duties to which he looked forward. His whole course of life was rudely interrupted when, at the age of twenty-five (597 B.C.), he was taken as captive to Babylonia by Nebuchadnezzar; cut off from every hope of becoming an active priest, it must have seemed to the young man that life had lost all meaning. We must never forget that when the epigram declares, "Jeremiah was a prophet who happened to be a priest; Ezekiel was a priest who happened to be a prophet," it is stating a real truth, even though expressed with typical epigrammatic exaggeration.

At first Ezekiel may have nourished hopes of an early return to the temple in Jerusalem (Jer. 29: 8f), but Jeremiah's letter and the fate of Ahab and Zedekiah (Jer. 29: 21ff) will have shown him that there was no hope that he would ever serve the Lord as priest in His temple. The greater, then, must have been his spiritual distress when he became thirty and realized with renewed force how the sin of his people had cut him off from his spiritual heritage.[1]

It was under such circumstances that God revealed Himself to Ezekiel (1: 1) and showed him that he was to fulfil his priestly vocation by acting as His prophet.

The Call of Ezekiel (1: 1—3: 21).

In the height of summer 592 B.C., Ezekiel was transported in a trance (3: 12, 14) to the banks of the river Chebar, a canal

---

[1] This interpretation of "the thirtieth year" is widely denied, but those who do so have nothing adequate to offer in its place. The one objection of weight is that a birthday could hardly be so referred to; apart from a few cases of royalty, the Bible ignores birthdays and is concerned merely with birthyears.

south of Babylon. As he stood there he saw a great storm-cloud being borne down on him out of the North (1: 4). As it drew nearer he saw that it was the chariot-throne of God (1: 5–28). We shall make no effort either to clarify Ezekiel's description or to expound its symbolism. For the former, recourse should be had to a commentary, if the study is felt to be profitable. As regards the latter, seeing that the rabbis themselves declared that he who had come to understand the Chariot knew all the mysteries of creation, and restricted its study to those over thirty, it is clear that for them, too, the symbolism presented the very greatest difficulties.

Ezekiel no more explains the living creatures or cherubim (10: 20) than Isaiah the seraphim (Isa. 6: 2); for us to attempt the task would lead us far beyond the limits of this book (but see note on 28: 14 below). Note that in 41: 19, probably for ease in reproduction, the cherubim have only two faces.

It is widely claimed by scholars that the cherubim of the vision show strong traces of the winged figures so common in Mesopotamian temples. While we consider the claim to be exaggerated, we have no interest in denying it. In the vision, the Chariot comes from the North, though Jehovah's residence in Zion is to the West (10: 4, 19; 11: 23; 43: 2ff). The simplest explanation is that the home of the Babylonian gods was in the North (Isa. 14: 13). If the Chariot comes from the North, it is because Jehovah has met and defeated the gods of Babylonia on their own ground; if the bearers of His Chariot remind us of the Babylonian temple guardians, it is because they have become His slaves. We are not suggesting that Ezekiel believed in the objective existence of the Babylonian deities, but simply that in such symbolical visions the details may carry implications which are far from obvious at first consideration.

If we find Ezekiel's symbolism over-elaborate and far-fetched, we must not forget that the whole of the priestly ritual was symbolic, as indeed was the lay-out of the Temple, and so symbolism had become second nature to him. It is essential for our study of Ezekiel to remember this, and also to bear in mind that there are Christians for whom Ezekiel is one of the most precious of the books of the Old Testament just because of its symbolism. The greatest difficulty of ch. 1 lies in the fact that when it comes to the glories of Deity, symbolism is as inadequate as direct description, and more difficult.

Ezekiel's Commissioning.

Ezekiel is addressed as Son of man (2: 1, and often elsewhere). This cannot be equated with the title "The Son of

Man," which our Lord used for Himself; it means no more than "man."

In 2: 3–7 Ezekiel is introduced to those to whom he is to prophesy, "nations that are rebellious" (ver. 3, so R.V.), *i.e.* both Judah and Israel. As the term "Judah" is very seldom used in Ezekiel, it is clear that "the House of Israel" and "the Children of Israel" refer in the first place to the Southern Kingdom, unless the context clearly shows otherwise. It is therefore far from clear how far Ezekiel's message was consciously addressed to the Northern exiles at all. Since Ezekiel was of the tribe of Levi, the term Israel was the more natural one for him: cf. the very similar use in Jeremiah. At first Ezekiel is given no clear indication of the result of his message, though the language is certainly not optimistic.

There follows a symbolic description of the source of his message and inspiration (2: 8–3: 3). His great prophetic predecessors felt themselves too much in the confidence of God to have used such a picture, but there is none that more clearly and forcefully shows the union of divine and human in the prophetic message. It is clearly divine, from God—this is symbolized by the already written roll. But the prophet does not merely deliver it to his hearers; he must first digest and assimilate it, making it a living part of himself. This is the human part of his message. The roll contained only "lamentations, mourning and woe" because there was a virtual recommissioning (33: 1–20) before Ezekiel began his work of upbuilding and comfort.

It is then (3: 4–11) made clear that the rebellious nations are the House of Israel, and that he will not be listened to. The Holy Spirit by returning him to his home (3: 12–15) shows him that his message is to be addressed particularly to the exiles there.

As he sits mute among his old surroundings for a week (3: 15) the word of the Lord comes to him again (3: 16–21) and makes it clear to him that his task is first and foremost that of watchman over the souls of the exiles. This is reinforced by the repetition and expansion of this commission just before the news of the destruction of Jerusalem reached the exiles (33: 1–20, 21) with the resultant change in the content of his prophecies. Ezekiel is above all the pastoral prophet, the priest watching over the souls entrusted to him.

To Whom Did Ezekiel Prophesy?

The interpretation given above would seem to be the obvious one, but in recent years it has been vigorously challenged, even by conservatives.[1] It is said that chs. 4–24 are

[1] A survey of modern views on Ezek. may be found in Bentzen: *Introduction to the Old Testament II*, p. 122 *seq.*

addressed exclusively to the inhabitants of Jerusalem, and that it is unprecedented for such prophecies to be spoken at a distance rather than face to face. There is not even a suggestion that they were sent in writing to distant Judaea. It is further claimed that certain passages presuppose Ezekiel's presence in Jerusalem (*e.g.* 5: 2; 11: 4–9, 13; 12: 2; 20: 30f). Ezekiel's message is to the House of Israel and the Children of Israel (2: 3), and it is said that these terms are in fact consistently used of those still in Jerusalem (but cf. 11: 15; 37: 16). Pfeiffer goes so far as to say that the view that Ezekiel remained in Tel-Abib "turns Ezekiel into a Jonah who failed to obey the divine command, 'Go, get thee unto the house of Israel'."[1]

The great objections to this view are that it does not explain how Ezekiel came to express himself so badly that men have misinterpreted his prophecy for centuries; that it is impossible to reconstruct the prophet's movements with any certainty; that a certain amount of re-arrangement of the text seems to be demanded. It should be noted that many of the references to the House of Israel suit the exiles just as well and sometimes better than those still living in Jerusalem.

Though we have rejected this view as unfounded, we believe it does furnish a clue to the understanding of chs. 4–24. We entirely agree with Pfeiffer's inability to accept Cooke's judgment, "No doubt we find it difficult to adjust ourselves to the position of a prophet in Babylonia hurling his denunciations at the inhabitants of Jerusalem across 700 miles of desert."[2] Such a picture seems to us mildly ridiculous. But we do not believe that these prophecies were either spoken to or intended for Jerusalem.

Ezekiel is the pastoral prophet; his task is the building up of God's new community. Jer. 24 gives both God's purpose for those taken into captivity with Jehoiachin and the popular explanation of their exile, a view that will have been shared by the exiles themselves. Before the prophet could begin his building up (chs. 33–48), he had to bring the exiles to a proper understanding of the principles that were leading God to hand over Jerusalem to destruction. How well he succeeded in making some of the exiles realize their high calling may be discovered by the attentive student of Ezra and Nehemiah.

The phrases taken to imply Ezekiel's presence in Jerusalem can be adequately explained by the extraordinary vividness of his trance visions, and by the symbolism that colours his whole message.

[1] *Introduction to the Old Testament*, p. 536.

[2] *Ibid.* p. 536 quoting Cooke: Ezekiel (I.C.C.), p. xxiiif.

Our interpretation also explains why there is nothing in Ezekiel that would even hint at Jeremiah's contemporary activities. We may well suppose that one so imbued with the priestly outlook as Ezekiel must have found Jeremiah's root and branch condemnation of ritual and ceremonial rather painful at times. But it seems impossible to believe that had Ezekiel actually prophesied in Jerusalem or even sent his messages there, he would not have sought to strengthen the hands of the older prophet, so hated and so lonely.

A Prophet Restrained (3: 22–27).

It would seem that a short interval is to be assumed between this and the previous section, during which Ezekiel's message had met serious opposition. Now God commands him to abstain from public ministry (ver. 24). Since the exiles would oppose him—the language of ver. 25 is probably to be taken figuratively of the restraint of bitter opposition, rather than of physical restraint—God would match restraint with restraint (ver. 26) by making the prophet dumb, though from time to time he would be able to speak (ver. 27).

This is a suitable point for considering one of the major problems of interpretation in Ezekiel. Ezekiel's dumbness is mentioned again in 24: 27; 29: 21; 33: 22; on the other hand, there are passages where it is virtually denied, *e.g.* 14: 4; 17: 2f, 12; 19: 1; 20: 3, etc. In ch. 4 he is described as lying on his side for 430 (or 390, cf. ver. 9) days, bound with cords (ver. 8), unless indeed this verse implies some form of paralysis; yet at the same time he is pressing the siege of Jerusalem with his model (4: 1–3) and also for 390 days making cakes and eating them, measuring his water and doing other actions apparently incompatible with his physical position. That these are not to be taken as happening consecutively is seen from the chronology. Between 1: 2 and 8: 1 are only 413 days, or 443, if it was a leap year of 13 months.

Once we realize that a completely literal interpretation of 4: 1–5: 4 is impossible, and link this fact with Ezekiel's extreme symbolism, we shall be prepared to recognize a metaphorical or symbolical element in the language used. Ezekiel's dumbness may mean no more than the absence of any prophetic message for considerable periods of time. The actions of 4: 1–5: 4 need only have been carried out at such times as he had visitors, or may even, though less likely, have been lived out purely in the prophet's mind. On the other hand, the extremely vivid trance-visions may point to some abnormality in Ezekiel's make-up.

The use of dried cow's dung (4: 15) for fuel is common in countries where other forms of fuel are scarce.

The Coming Doom of Jerusalem (Chs. 4–7).

These acted prophecies date about four and a half years before the final siege of Jerusalem began, and indeed before Zedekiah's fatal rebellion.

The figure in 4: 9 suggests that there were only 390 days in all for Ezekiel to lie on his side, the 40 for Judah being coalesced with the 390 for Israel. It seems impossible to find any adequate interpretation for the figures. To "bear their iniquity" means to bear the punishment for their iniquity. But in spite of 29: 11–14, it cannot be maintained that Ezekiel placed the duration of the exile at forty years. Jer. 29: 10, written earlier, would have prevented that. Perhaps the forty years are merely symbolic, reminiscent of the forty years in the wilderness. It has been pointed out that if we subtract the forty years from the 390, the remaining 350 are in round numbers the period from the disruption of the kingdom under Rehoboam to the time of Ezekiel. We do not, however, put these suggestions forward with any degree of confidence. The difficulty here should serve as a warning against any over-confidence in the interpretation of Ezekiel's symbolism.

Since it was forbidden to sow a field with more than one kind of grain (Lev. 19: 19; Deut. 22: 9) it may be that bread made from a mixture of grain was also unclean (4: 9).

The explanation of the symbolic actions follows in 5: 5–17. Note at this stage the vagueness about the sins involved, and that they are summed-up in the defilement of the sanctuary (5: 11). Ezekiel can wax indignant about social wrongs, but as a priest he sees the sins of the people particularly from the ritual angle.

The thought is continued in ch. 6, a prophecy against the idolatrous high places (the mountains) of Israel, *i.e.* especially Judah. Note that here it is the mere fact of idolatry rather than its consequences that is being condemned.

The section closes with a dirge (ch. 7) over the land of Israel, *i.e.* the kingdom of Judah.

The Desecration of the Temple (Ch. 8).

The second group of prophecies begins with a long trance-vision (chs. 8–11). The presence of the elders (ver. 1) suggests that whatever the original opposition to Ezekiel as prophet, it had rapidly passed, at least among the leaders of the people. It is probably this respect, paid perhaps more to the priest than the prophet, that made it possible for Ezekiel's prophecies to assume a much longer and more rounded form than did those of his predecessors.

The significance of their presence is that they are able to

vouch for the reality of Ezekiel's trance. It may be that as the
vision developed Ezekiel described aloud what he was seeing.

In ver. 2 we should read with the LXX "a likeness as the
appearance of a man." Ezekiel's symbolism comes out once
more in ver. 3 by the mention of the form of a hand, for his
transportation is by virtue of the spirit. There are certainly
symbolic elements in what follows as well. Ezekiel sees
four forms of idolatry which implicitly cover the whole people.

(*a*) The image which made Jehovah jealous (ver. 3ff),
placed at the north, or popular entrance to the inner court.
This probably was an image of Jehovah Himself, and represented that popular Canaanization of Jehovah-worship that
was the curse of Israel from the time of the Judges on (see
p. 36ff). The making of such pictorial representations is one
of the things that moved Jehovah to jealousy (Exod. 20: 4f;
Deut. 4: 23f; 5: 8f). The image is purely symbolic here.

(*b*) A multitude of heathen idols, mostly foreign (vers. 6–
12). This is probably entirely symbolic (see vers. 8, 12) and
speaks of the aping of heathen religion, probably mainly
Egyptian and Babylonian, by the leaders of the people, the
elders (ver. 11, R.V.).

(*c*) The Canaanite fertility cult (ver. 14f), which appealed
particularly to the women (cf. Jer. 7: 18; 44: 15–19). Tam-
muz (the Greek Adonis) was one of the most popular gods of
this fertility cult, having different names and characteristics
at different times and in different countries. Here he is the
god of vegetation, killed off by the drought and heat of summer. So Ezekiel sees him being mourned in August.

(*d*) Sun worship (vers. 15–18) by the priests—because the
worshippers stand between the temple and the altar (ver. 16).
The offence is the worse because they stand with their backs to
the sanctuary. They have added to all their social iniquity
this blatant challenge to Jehovah (ver. 17), and even "thrust
their branch into My face" (lit., nose)—the present Hebrew
text "their nose" is according to valid rabbinic tradition a
scribal alteration out of respect to God.

The Divine Judgment (9: 1–11: 13).

Chs. 9 and 10, and possibly even 11: 13, are symbolically
prophetic, for the rebellion against Nebuchadnezzar had not
even broken out yet. The instruments of judgment are
obviously angels, though always called men. That the
apostasy was not universal is shown by the marking of the
faithful on their foreheads (9: 4). The Hebrew for "mark"
is *tav*, the name of the last letter of the alphabet, which in the
old script was a cross.

Then follows the slaying of the unmarked (9: 5–11), which

the intercession of the prophet is powerless to avert. God makes it clear that it is not so much the idolatry that brings the judgment, as the social iniquity, bloodshed and wresting of judgment (9: 9, R.V.), based on the belief that Nebuchadnezzar's success meant that Jehovah had forsaken the land (R.V. mg.). Then the coals of divine wrath from the altar on the chariot-throne of God are scattered on the doomed city (ch. 10), though the prophet does not see their effect.

Special judgment is pronounced on the men who were plotting rebellion against Babylon, and the death of one of them (almost certainly real, not symbolic) prefigures the fate of all (11: 1–13). They were daring and cynical men, with their metaphor "this city is the caldron, and we be the flesh." They meant that though their course of action would make things hot for them, the fortifications of the city would save them from the flames of destruction. God tells them that the only flesh left in the city will be corpses; they themselves will be dragged out and executed by the Chaldeans.

God's Grace to the Exiles (11: 14–25).

We have already referred to the attitude of those left in the land to the exiles (see p. 91). Here it comes out again in a cruel and blatant form (ver. 15). They pictured the exiles as far from Jehovah, but He would be to them a sanctuary (*i.e.* a temple) for a little while (ver. 16, R.V.),[1] and would then bring them back to the land. The fruit of the exile should be changed natures. For "one heart" (ver. 19) we should almost certainly read "another heart" with the LXX, or "a new heart" with the Syriac and 18: 31; 36: 26. In either case the change in Hebrew is small.

The glory of God had been gradually leaving the defiled temple and city, cf. 8: 4; 9: 3; 10: 19. Now (ver. 23) it leaves the city altogether. The fact that it leaves the city eastward may well suggest that it was going to lodge among the exiles (cf. ver. 16).

Zedekiah's Fate (12: 1–20).

We are now back in Tel-Abib, and the prophet by two symbolic actions (vers. 3–7, 17f) foreshadows the fate both of the prince, *i.e.* Zedekiah, and of the people.

The title "prince" (*nasi*) is outside Ezekiel only applied to Solomon among kings, and the passage (I Kings 11: 34) gives the clue to its use here; Solomon had forfeited his right to be king. For Ezekiel, the Judaean kingship had ended with Jehoiachin's exile. For the use of "prince" in the closing chapters of Ezekiel, see below.

The symbolic action is in itself deliberately absurd, so as to

---

[1] Even better, "a sanctuary in small measure." cf. my *Ezekiel*, p. 48.

catch the attention of the people. Ezekiel was to carry out of his house the little bundle of goods a man would take with him into exile (ver. 4, R.V. mg.). Then in the evening he was to take it back into the house, dig through the wall (built as always in Babylonia of sun-dried bricks), bring out his bundle, wrap his face up so that he could not see, and stagger off with his bundle. The application (vers. 10–13) is clear in the light of its fulfilment; Zedekiah's flight by night (II Kings 25: 4), his capture, blinding and leading into exile (II Kings 25: 5ff).

The second symbolic action, in which Ezekiel eats his meals, carefully weighing the quantities and in great fear, is little more than an extension of 4: 9–17.

On Prophecy and the Prophets (12: 21—13: 23).

Though a large part of his predecessors' prophecies had gone into fulfilment, enough still remained unfulfilled to create the same attitude in men's hearts that we find in II Pet. 3: 4. To them Ezekiel has to make clear that the storm will break in their day (12: 21–28) and that it will sweep away the false prophets (12: 24).

Ezekiel then turns on the false prophets. He condemns them first (13: 1–9) for following "their own spirit, and things which they have not seen" (ver. 3, mg.). Then (13: 10–16) he charges them with whitewashing, *i.e.* giving their approbation to the jerry-built walls of man's making (see mg. ver. 10). Finally, he condemns the prophetesses (13: 17–23). It is impossible now to know with certainty what the rigmaroles of these women meant. This in turn makes our rendering of the Hebrew uncertain. This passage is important as showing the danger of arguing from silence. If we did not have it, we might assume that the prophetess, whether good or bad, was a rare phenomenon in Israel.

The Inevitable Penalty of Idolatry (Chs. 14–16).

These chapters are introduced by certain of the leaders of the exiles coming to Ezekiel for prophetic guidance (14: 1ff). God refuses them an answer, because they are idolaters, except the answer of destruction (14: 4–8). Should any other answer come, it is because the prophet has allowed himself to be enticed by the idolaters, and he will suffer the same fate (14: 9ff). So terrible is idolatry that the presence of righteous men means only that they themselves will be saved (14: 12–23). For Daniel see p. 142; note that the spelling of the name in Hebrew here and in 28: 3 is not the same as in the book of Daniel.

The warning is reinforced by the example of the vine (ch. 15) which has value only as it produces grapes. From the

time of Isaiah (Isa. 5: 1–7), if not before, the vine had been used
as a symbol for Israel. The only fruit it had produced was wild
grapes, and now both ends had been burnt and the middle
had been charred (this is the force of "burned," ver. 4), so
there was no future for it but to be burnt up.

Ezekiel then gives the spiritual history of Israel in a powerful allegory of the foundling child who becomes the faithless
wife of her benefactor (ch. 16). Lack of space makes any
effort to expound the superabundant symbolism impossible.
Of outstanding importance, however, are the closing thoughts
of the chapter (vers. 46–63). Jerusalem's sins are much
greater than those of Sodom and Samaria (cf. Jer. 3: 6–13).
Since there is to be a restoration of Jerusalem, how much more
of rebellious Samaria, and heathen Sodom, symbolizing probably the small heathen nations round Israel.

It should be noted that there are really two allegories; the
foundling child (16: 1–43), and the two sisters (16: 44–52).
We then have the restoration of the sisters (16: 53–59) and final
reconciliations (16: 60–63).

The Folly and Treachery of Zedekiah (Ch. 17).

God evidently revealed to Ezekiel Zedekiah's first moves
that were to lead to his open rebellion against Babylon. Ezekiel
tells a parable that is a riddle in its obscurity (vers. 1–10). In
its interpretation he especially stresses the evil of Zedekiah's
broken oath (vers. 13f, 16). This prophecy concludes with the
parabolic promise (ver. 22ff) that from the descendants of those
transported to Babylon with Jehoiachin there will be a restoration. The language of ver. 22f seems Messianic,[1] but in the
light of Jer. 22: 29f we must be cautious. Our Lord was only
officially a descendant of Jehoiachin (Matt. 1: 2–16).

The Citizen Basis of the Restored Community (Ch. 18).

Both Jeremiah and Ezekiel lived in a time when men were
reaping the whirlwind of the storm their ancestors had sown.
There seemed no point in individual effort, for a man's fate
would be the same whether he fought against the current or
swam with the tide. Their pessimism was summed up in the
proverb, "The fathers have eaten sour grapes and the children's teeth are blunted" (Jer. 31: 29; Ezek. 18: 2). As they
look to the future, both the prophets see a time when a man's
relationship to God will be essentially an individual one, not
to be influenced by either the goodness or badness of his people.
Jeremiah thinks more of the individual's standing with God;
Ezekiel, more of the reward or punishment of his actions.

This chapter has suffered grievously at the hand of those

[1] For a more careful discussion see my *Ezekiel*, p. 69f.

that have wished to interpret it against the background of the New Testament. It is not in contradiction to the Gospel, because Ezekiel is standing on the foundation of the Law. But he is shifting the operation of the Law from the nation and family to the individual. Quite typical of Ezekiel is the mixture of religious, ethical and ceremonial in his list of sins and virtues (vers. 6–9).

The section ends with a lament over the kings of Judah: Jehoahaz (19: 1–4), Jehoiakim-Jehoiachin, probably considered as one (19: 5–9), Zedekiah (19: 10–14).

The Deeper Meaning of the Sin (Chs. 20–23).

These chapters, which cover the period between the open breach of Zedekiah with Babylon and the appearing of the Chaldean army under the walls of Jerusalem, in many ways parallel much of the previous main section. But we feel the prophetic voice probing deeper. In ch. 22 the sins of Jerusalem are seen more clearly and in darker colours. Then ch. 20 is one of the most important in the Old Testament for its estimate of Israelite history as a whole, with its contrast between Israel's consistent disobedience from the beginning, and Jehovah acting throughout for His name's sake.

20: 25f has an historical interest. It was used by the early Hebrew-Christians, and by some Gentile Christians, in their controversy with the Synagogue, to prove that the sacrificial system was not God-given. However, in the light of chs. 40–48 any such interpretation would seem self-contradictory. The obvious interpretation of ver. 26 is that the statutes referred to human sacrifice (cf. Jer. 7: 31). But it is out of the question that Ezekiel should attribute such sacrifices to God. So the most reasonable interpretation is that God deliberately worded His law in such a way that the rebellious and unspiritual misunderstood it.

Imminent Judgment (Ch. 24).

On the very day (ver. 1f; II Kings 25: 1) that the Chaldean armies appeared before the walls of Jerusalem, Ezekiel received his final message of doom in which he saw Jerusalem as a great rusty caldron (so R.V.) in which the contents are boiled up and thrown out, and then the caldron is burnt out in the flames.

Later at an unspecified time, but quite possibly on the day when Jerusalem fell, God tells Ezekiel that his wife is to die, but he is not to mourn her (ver. 15ff). When she dies the same evening the people ask Ezekiel why he does not mourn. He tells them that this is but a picture of what will happen when the news of Jerusalem's fall comes to them.

Prophecies Against the Nations (Chs. 25–32).

These prophecies have the same general purpose as those against the nations in Isaiah and Jeremiah, the setting of God's judgments on Israel against the general background of God's judgments on the world. There is probably a symbolic element here as well, Tyre being chosen as representing godless commerce, and Egypt for the grossness of its idolatry (cf. 16: 26, which cannot be taken literally). This element may perhaps partly explain the suspended fulfilments we referred to in ch. I.

In certain circles it is accepted as axiomatic that 28: 11–19 refers to Satan and his fall. However attractive this view, we would point out that it makes no attempt to explain the setting of the oracle; it takes it out of its context. In addition it should be noted that the rabbis never so understood it, so it is not so obvious as some think. The question is further complicated by many textual and linguistic problems in the passage. It is generally overlooked that this view tacitly attributes to cherub (28: 14) a meaning that is not readily discoverable in other Scripture references. In spite of all the difficulties involved, we believe that the prophecy does refer to the king of Tyre, though we believe that as a picture of human pride it may be used like Isa. 14: 4–21 as a type of Satan.

Advocates of soul sleep are given to using 32: 17–32 as a proof that in the Old Testament *Sheol* is in all respects equivalent to the grave. Those who have tried to grapple with the problems of Ezekiel's symbolism are not likely to take this unique passage literally. A doctrine needs a more positive basis than a passage like this will afford.

The Prophet's Recommissioning (Ch. 33).

As Ezekiel waited for the certain fulfilment of his prophecy of doom on Jerusalem, God recommissioned him as watchman over the House of Israel (vers. 1–9; cf. 3: 16–21). Though we are not so told, it is likely that it was accompanied by a vision of the chariot-throne of God. God's charge is accompanied by a message (vers. 10–20) very reminiscent of ch. 18. In its setting, however, it seems to stress above all that the exiles were facing a new beginning, when each had to make his individual choice, whether he would do the will of God or not.

Jerusalem fell on the ninth day of the fourth month in Zedekiah's eleventh year (Jer. 39: 2), and the temple was burnt on the seventh day of the following month (II Kings 25: 8f). About six months later rumours in Tel-Abib were silenced by the arrival of one of the survivors (ver. 21). [The Hebrew text says that it was about eighteen months later, but this is

intrinsically absurd. Some MSS. as well as the Syriac translation have "in the eleventh year," which is obviously correct.]

Ezekiel had been prepared for the fugitive's coming by the
removal of his dumbness (ver. 22), which if our earlier explanation is correct, means that from now on he was able at all
times to proclaim and explain the will of God. With his
changed task came also the realization that the remnant in
Judaea had not been changed even by the destruction of Jerusalem (vers. 23–29, cf. Jer. 40–45); he was also reminded that
his increasing popularity was no evidence that the majority of
the people were willing to accept his message (vers. 30–33).
No account is given us of the details of Ezekiel's later work,
and no indication is given as to when the following chapters
were spoken, or to what extent they are a summary of years of
teaching.

Rulers past and future (Ch. 34).

For the correct understanding of this chapter it must be
remembered that metaphorically the shepherd always means
the king, whether it is used of God or man. Our understanding of this has been obscured by the religious connotation
given to "pastor" in the Christian Church. Elders in the
Church are under-shepherds, for they bear rule as the Spirit-
appointed delegates of Jesus Christ, "the Chief Shepherd," and
"the good Shepherd," the Ruler and King of the Church (I
Pet. 5: 1–4). What the implications of true rule are, this
chapter shows (vers. 11–22).

Ezekiel clearly implies that the destruction of Jerusalem
and the exile do not mark a merely temporary interruption
in the rule of the Davidic house. For an indeterminate period
Israel is to have no other king than Jehovah Himself (ver. 11.
seq.). Only then will the Davidic line be restored in the person
of the Messianic king (ver. 23). In contrast to chs. 12: 10; 19:
1; 21: 25 no stress may be laid on the fact that he is called
"prince" (*nasi*, ver. 24), for in 37: 24 he is called king. Rather
the title is used to underline that the return to the Davidic
kingship will not obscure the kingship of Jehovah.

Ver. 17 should be rendered: "Behold, I judge between
sheep and sheep, even the rams and the he-goats." The rams
and the he-goats explain the second "sheep." They are the
rich and the strong who took advantage of bad and selfish
kingship to oppress the poor and weak.

The Restored Land (Chs. 35, 36).

Though Ezekiel is undoubtedly speaking about the land in
a literal sense, it should be obvious that he uses it symbolically
as well. Jehovah's ownership of the mountains of Israel is

stressed, for His attitude toward them symbolizes His attitude toward all that is peculiarly His.

First, God's punishment on Edom is announced (ch. 35). Edom symbolizes all who hate (vers. 5, 11; cf. Amos 1: 11; Obad. 10–12; Ps. 137: 7) that which is God's. Edom's sin was the worse because, unlike Assyria (Isa. 10: 5f), and Babylon (Isa. 47: 6), he had never been commissioned by Jehovah to act against Israel. So we can easily see why Edom is singled out (cf. Isa. 34, p. 53). Then Ezekiel proclaims the complete freeing of the land from intrusive nations (36: 1–7), and its restoration to the fruitfulness which had been God's original purpose for it (36: 8–15).

Entirely in line with Isaiah's use of the transformation of nature, it is then made clear (36: 16–38) that even as the desolation of the land was due to the sins of its inhabitants, so its restoration involves their transformation. In what is the climax of his prophecy (vers. 24–27) Ezekiel makes clear the implications of Jer. 31: 31–34). God's new people must be one inwardly transformed. As in Jeremiah, great stress is laid on its being God's action done purely in grace.

The Restored People (Ch. 37).

Though the language of the vision (vers. 1–14) presupposes a belief in resurrection, it should be clear that it is not the resurrection of dead Israelites that is here under consideration, but the revival of the nation. This is borne out by the gradual reconstruction and resuscitation of the dead bodies. The mention of the opening of their graves (ver. 12f) is explained by "I will bring you into the land of Israel." An application to a national revival of Israel, which will at the same time be a spiritual one, seems inescapable. While dogmatism is out of place, he would be a bold man who would categorically deny that we are seeing the beginnings of fulfilment to-day.

The English obscures the fact that the Hebrew uses the same word for "breath" (vers. 5, 6, 8, 9, 10) and "wind" (ver. 9), while in either case it could be rendered by "spirit."

National revival presupposes national unity, and in vers. 15–28 this is represented symbolically. The translation "stick" (ver. 16), though linguistically justifiable, misses the meaning. It is the ruler's staff or rod that is meant. The uniting of the rods means that there will be only one king over them (ver. 22).

Though "the children of Israel" (which includes Judah) in ver. 21 seems to suggest that Ezekiel is thinking primarily of those from the Northern Kingdom that had gone into exile, the possibility cannot be ruled out that he is referring to those left in the land (cf. ch. XI on Jer. 2: 1–4: 4). This raises a matter which can only be mentioned, but not discussed, here. There are a number of prophetic passages which foretell the restoration of the Northern tribes, *e.g.* Hos. 3: 4f; 14; Isa. 11: 13; Jer. 31: 1–9, etc. While we personally are convinced that the Jews of to-day contain within their number representatives of all the tribes, yet we equally do not feel that this can be regarded in any way as an adequate fulfilment of such prophecies. Unfortunately the topic is normally dealt with either by what seems to us hardly legitimate treatment of both the Scriptures and history, or is virtually ignored. May it be that the conditional element enters in here too? Did Judah in exile make the response God demanded, while the older exiles of the North refused? It may be, for the topic hardly seems to find a mention in the New Testament. This uncertainty shows, however, that much dogmatism on far more abstruse matters is hard to justify.

The Last Enemies (Chs. 38, 39).

Instead of letting themselves be guided by Rev. 20: 7ff, many prophetic expositors have been misled by the apparent relationship of these chapters to ch. 40 *seq.*, and have placed ch. 38f first in time. Between 33: 21 and 40: 1 over twelve or thirteen years elapse (see above on ch. 33). If Josephus is to be trusted, chs. 40–48 may very well originally have appeared as a separate book. It is therefore much wiser to see in ch. 38f the great final rebellion against God foretold in Rev. 20: 7ff. This seems to be borne out by verses like 38: 8, 11, 12, 14, 17.

We do not intend to discuss the various identifications of the names in these chapters. It seems, however, most in keeping both with the general language of these chapters, and with the symbolic nature of the book in general, to look upon them not so much as a definite prophecy of identifiable nations, but rather as symbolic names for the nations at the ends of the earth.

39: 25 is not necessarily in conflict with the above tentative explanation. "I will bring again the captivity of Jacob" has no linguistic connexion with "went into captivity" (39: 23). A far more probable translation is: "I will restore the fortunes of Jacob."

Contrary to popular exegesis, Sheba, Dedan, and the merchants of Tarshish, so far from opposing the unprovoked assault, seem to be eager to share in the spoils (38: 13).

Ezekiel's vision of the restored community ends with the Spirit of God on the House of Israel (39: 29), which is therefore a transformed community.

H

The People at Peace (Chs. 40–48).

Reference has already been made to the possibility that these chapters may originally have been published by themselves. Certainly they form a unique unit within Ezekiel. Though the usual view is that they should be taken literally— this is irrespective of whether a fulfilment is expected—there are serious grounds for questioning it. No one who takes them literally doubts that we are dealing with a Millennial scene.[1] But the whole concept of a Millennial temple of this type raises serious difficulties. At the present moment there is no spot preferable to another for prayer and worship. To us it seems incredible that the Millennium would mean a spiritually retrograde step. This applies, too, to the confinement of priesthood to a group chosen by birth.

From the literalist side no satisfactory explanation has ever been given for the reintroduction of sacrifices, and the difficulty becomes particularly acute when we find the sin offering (43: 19–25; 45: 17, 18–25—note that the prince has to bring a sin-offering, 45: 22). The suggestion that they are mere memorial sacrifices looking back to the Cross is without support in the section itself, and fails to meet the objection that, if bread and wine suffice now, how much less should the sacrifice of animals be necessary then. The prince (44: 3; 45: 7f, 16f, 22–25; 46: 2–12, 16ff)—he is never called king—is little more than a superintender of the services, and bears no resemblance to the Messianic king of prophecy.

Finally, it seems imperative to regard the river of 47: 1–12 as symbolic. Quite apart from the fact that it flows out of the peak of a very high mountain (40: 2; 47: 1), it deepens miraculously. No appeal may be made to tributaries, for the whole point is that this is holy water. Much the same must be said of the division of the land.

Once we grasp that there is symbolism in these chapters, we should not be daunted by our inability to understand much of it (cf. the opening vision), but should be rather prepared to see the whole as primarily symbolic. A redeemed people, among whom Jehovah dwells (43: 2–5; 48: 35), cannot be organized haphazardly. In even the smallest details of life and organization the will of God must be done; this is the message of these chapters.

Naturally, Ezekiel is thinking of a restored Israel, a rebuilt temple, and a perfectly kept law. But in the prophet's vision the type loses itself in the fulfilment, the shadow in the substance, the earthly in the heavenly. Both the present and the

---

[1] Those who see in these chapters Ezekiel's blue prints for the restored community hold that Ezekiel saw in the promised restoration the setting up of the kingdom of God.

Millennium, the Israel of God and the Church of God, the earthly and the heavenly Jerusalem, the law written on tablets of stone and on men's hearts, blend together in a unique combination of literalism and symbolism. While the future will never see a purely literal fulfilment, the present witnesses, partially, the spiritual fulfilment.

Prophecy and Apocalyptic.

As the Hebrew prophet looks further and further into the future, the clear-cut lines of his picture become blurred. This may be by the background becoming hazy, or even virtually vanishing. This is particularly the case in Messianic prophecy —note especially the timeless background of the Servant Songs in Isaiah (see p. 58). On the other hand, the whole picture may lose its sharp outlines; Isa. 24–27 is an excellent example of this. Again, we find the use of stock expressions, verging on the symbolic, or even passing over into it; Ezek. 38f, is a good example of this.

In Ezek. 40–48, however, we are introduced to a new form of prophecy. The first peculiarity is that it is *entirely* in vision form. Then, the personal rôle of the prophet is, apparently at least, diminished. He becomes the recorder of what he sees and of the explanations given him. What is yet more important is that the prophet's guide and mentor is an angelic being, and not directly God. When we add to this the symbolic nature of much of the vision, if not of all, we shall realize that this is something new.

Zech. 1–8 are mixed, but on the whole they carry the tendencies of the closing chapters of Ezekiel even further. But it is in Dan. 7–12 that this form of prophecy reaches its Old Testament climax. Here the application is taken out of the prophet's own time, for the vision is for the time of the end, and until then the words are to be shut up and sealed (Dan. 8: 26; 12: 4, 9). To distinguish this form of prophecy from that usually found in the prophetic books, it is normally called apocalyptic.

Daniel was a prophet (Matt. 24: 15), but prophecy stretches from a prophet's concern with the daily details of life (cf. I Sam. 9: 6; I Kings 14: 1ff; etc.) through the proclamation of the eternal principles of the unchanging God to the mysterious foretelling of the distant future. Just as the first only receives casual mention, so the last, as represented by Daniel, quite understandably and correctly, finds its place in the Hebrew canon in the Writings and not in the Prophets.

The place of Daniel in the Jewish canon is widely used as evidence that it must have been written after 200 B.C. "when the canon of the Prophets was closed." This argument overlooks the fact that the Jewish rabbi was just as capable of distinguishing between apocalyptic and normal prophecy as the modern scholar. Then, the fact that the place of Ezekiel in the canon was challenged as late as the end of the first century A.D. shows that "the closing" of the prophetic canon by 200 B.C. is merely a statement of historic fact, and not of a theory of prophetic inspiration. (Ezekiel was challenged because it seemed to be in contradiction to the Law—a difficulty resolved by Chananiah ben Hezekiah after burning 300 measures of midnight oil—and because it seemed to give a handle to certain gnostic speculations.)

CHAPTER XIV

HAGGAI

Post-exilic Prophecy.

JEWISH tradition confined recorded post-exilic prophecy to the contents of Haggai, Zechariah and Malachi, and this is the view adopted by us. Modern scholarship for the most part would add "Trito-Isaiah," Isa. 24–27, Joel and the moral tale of Jonah, as well as considerable additions in other prophets. Even were we to accept this, it would not materially alter our picture of post-exilic prophecy.

It seems to be clear that prophecy died out very largely because prophets were not really wanted. In Zech. 13: 2–6 we have the last miserable end of the professional prophets. Nehemiah was troubled by them (Neh. 6: 10–14), but it is striking that he reveals no sense of loss at the lack of genuine prophets. We can discover at least four reasons for the rapidly diminishing regard for the prophet.

(1) The religious Jew, apart from an exceptional crisis that might occur once in a life-time, had outgrown the need for some almost mechanical means for the discovery of God's will, whether through the priest with Urim and Thummim or the prophet through his dreams or clairvoyance. He had in large measure learnt that we can know God's will now through His self-revelation in the past. This was intensified by the post-exilic community's being a religious rather than a national community, as was the case before the exile. This was emphasized by the failure to obtain national independence until 142 B.C. The Jew who was not interested in his religion normally just did not return from Babylonia.

(2) The returning exiles contained an altogether disproportionate number of priests, Levites and ecclesiastical persons, a total of nearly 5,700 out of 42,360 (Ezra 2), a proportion of about 1 in 7½. Ezra is not so explicit about the numbers that returned with him, but we may be fairly sure that they were not strikingly dissimilar. The priest always tended to be suspicious of the prophet and to think himself his superior. It is therefore typical that when doubts arose as to the eligibility of some of the priests that had returned, the Tirshatha deferred the matter until "there stood up a priest with Urim and with Thummim" (Ezra 2: 62f). There is no

suggestion that a prophetic opinion, if offered, would have been acceptable. Quite consistently with this whole attitude we find that Zechariah was a priest, and Haggai and Malachi probably came from ecclesiastical circles. It is true that in I Macc. 4: 46; 14: 41 we have certain matters kept for prophetic decision in the future, but the context creates the impression that the prophet was not expected until Mal. 4: 5 was fulfilled. That the priest can be called the angel of Jehovah in Mal. 2: 7 (the English misleadingly, though accurately, for angel=messenger, renders "the messenger of the LORD") shows how the priesthood was now exalted.

(3) Ezra and to a less extent Nehemiah stamped on the post-exilic community the awareness that they were a people under the divine law; at the same time the story clearly suggests that Ezra was no innovator; he was merely giving expression to a principle already generally accepted. His underlying assumption, one that was bound to lead in due time to Pharisaism and Rabbinic Judaism, was that in the Law as interpreted by the prophets of the past all that man needed to know of God had been given. All that was needed was a mind filled with wisdom derived from the fear of the Lord. In such a society a prophet was an anachronism.

(4) Even if conditions had not been unpropitious for the prophets, it is likely that they would gradually have faded out, for their main work was done. God had said all through them in sundry ways and divers manners that could be said. Now the community had to learn and absorb what had been given them in the Law and the Prophets, that they might be prepared for Him who was the fulfilment of both the Law and the Prophets. Modern scholarship has done much to fill the gap between the Testaments, but the gap has its place in our Bibles; it was a time not of revelation but of learning and discipline.

The Historical Background of Haggai and Zechariah.

Though Cyrus was a man of most enlightened character, it was as a world conqueror that he impressed himself on the history of his time, and his conquest of Babylon in 539 B.C. was only an incident in continuous fighting that did not end until his death in the field in 530 B.C. Most of the short reign of Cambyses, his son (530–522 B.C.) was spent in the conquest and breaking of Egypt. So it was not until the reign of Darius I (522–486 B.C.) that the Persian empire was really organized.

It is easy then to see how the much stronger neighbours of the Jews found it easy to frustrate the decree of Cyrus about the rebuilding of the temple (Ezra 4: 4f), especially in the matter of covering the expenses (Ezra 6: 4). This worked in with the very real material difficulties the returned exiles had to face, and so they acquiesced saying, "It is not yet the time for the building of the house of Jehovah" (Hag. 1: 2). It is quite typical that the priestly Chronicler should mention only the outside opposition, the prophet Haggai only the inner unwillingness. The truth is a combination of both.

By the second year of Darius the main rebellions that threatened to rend the Persian empire asunder had been crushed, and it was clear that strong rule might be expected. The excuse of external opposition had now collapsed, and so the prophets Haggai and Zechariah arose to deal with the real spiritual reasons that had held up the rebuilding of the Temple. How right they were in ignoring the excuse of external opposition is seen by the fact that as soon as the rebuilding of the Temple was officially challenged (Ezra 5: 3), the central government reaffirmed and strengthened the original edict of Cyrus (Ezra 6: 6–12), which was then obeyed by the local authorities (Ezra 6: 13).[1]

The Prophet Haggai and His Message.

Though it is not explicitly stated, it is fairly universally assumed that Haggai was one of those that had returned from Babylonia. The section 2: 10–14 is so technical in its outlook that it is generally agreed that Haggai must either have been a priest or have belonged at least to the Temple circles. It may be that the non-mention of the name of his father points to the latter as shewing his family not to be of great importance.

It has been suggested by some that Haggai is rather pedestrian and that his message appeals to self-interest. Certainly his language cannot be compared with some of his predecessors; it is rhythmic prose not poetry, but it seems well wedded to the message.

As we showed above Haggai was speaking to men who had made great sacrifices for God, whose chief purpose was to serve God more perfectly. When God did not respond to the sanguine hopes with which they had returned, when they found themselves faced with great material problems and hampered in rebuilding by being refused the promised government aid, they naturally tended to ask whether they had misunderstood the will of Jehovah, and to suggest that the time

[1] The above picture of events is seriously challenged by a leading group of Old Testament scholars. As the subject is hardly relevant to the purpose of this book, and since the latest scholarly commentary on Ezr.-Neh. by Rudolph (in German) seems completely to support the main outline of the view given above, we see no point in discussing the matter. Those interested are referred to Oesterley & Robinson: *A History of Israel*, Vol. II, chs. VII, VIII.

for rebuilding had not yet come. Lack of faith and self-interest combined to create a plausible mask for their motives which deceived the majority.

Haggai pointed out first of all that their material distress had not been as great as they had persuaded themselves, for they had been able to "ciel," *i.e.* line with wood, their own houses (1: 4). In the hills of Judæa stone is cheap, wood is a luxury. Then with the same simple, stern logic shown by Amos, he pointed out (1: 5f) that they had not received even the minimum they might have expected, if they had been doing God's will. There could be only one logical reason—the neglect of the Temple (1: 9ff).

The promise of immediate material blessing (2: 15–19) is in no sense a bribe. It is part of Haggai's spiritual logic. Once a God-fearing people was doing God's will there could be only one result.

It may very well be this sense of spiritual logic rather than of revelation, though there are passages of prophetic revelation in the book, that caused Haggai to use the phrase "the word of Jehovah came *by* Haggai the prophet" (1: 1, 3; 2: 1, 10) instead of *to* Haggai as one would expect (cf. Jer. 1: 2; Ezek. 1: 3; Hos. 1: 1; Jonah 1: 1; Mic. 1: 1; Zeph. 1: 1; Zech. 1: 1, etc.). When it is a matter purely of revelation (2: 20–23) then the usual formula is used (2: 20).

The book is divided into four dated messages covering a period of little more than three months.

The First Message and the People's Response (Ch. 1).

To what extent the Temple had actually been destroyed by Nebuchadnezzar must remain an open question, but II Kings 25: 9 suggests little more than damage by fire, which would have left most of the stone-work in place. It is entirely consistent with this that while it took a wealthy king with all the resources of his kingdom at his disposal seven and a half years to build the original sanctuary (I Kings 6: 37f), the small body of impoverished people who had returned from Babylonia were able to do the bulk of the rebuilding in under four years (Ezra 6: 15; Hag. 1: 1). That is surely also the reason why Haggai lays chief stress on the timber needed (1: 8, cf. 1: 4).

The response of the people headed by Zerubbabel seems to have been quick. The interpretation of 1: 15 is not easy, for as it stands it seems to contradict 2: 18. The Hebrew separates it from the preceding, linking it with what follows, but this does not seem to make sense. The simplest explanation is that 1: 15 marks the date when the people began to collect material for building, 2: 18 the actual beginning of the work.

It is probable that 1: 13 should be translated: Then spake

Haggai, The Angel of the LORD *is here* with a message of the LORD for the people, saying, I am with you, saith the LORD. For the Angel of Jehovah see p. 125.

The Second Message (2: 1–9).

The view expressed above that much of the stone-work of the Temple had been left standing seems confirmed by ver. 3, for a comparison would not have been possible, if nothing had been left to compare. Haggai encourages the people by telling them:

(*a*) The "shaking" which brought down Babylon was not, as the exiles had hoped, the final one. Soon this final "shaking" would come, and then the house they were building would be there to welcome Jehovah as He set up His kingdom.

(*b*) Promises like that of Isa 56: 7 would see their fulfilment there. 2: 7 is only Messianic in the wider sense. The A.V. rendering "the desire of all nations" is based on the Vulgate and is incompatible with the Hebrew. We must either render as in the R.V. or perhaps better "the desired of all nations shall come," *i.e.* all the nations which Jehovah desires and chooses. Obviously for his hearers this implied the coming of the Messiah as well.

(*c*) The outward beautifying of the Temple could await God's giving (ver. 8). From His people at the time He asked no more than they could give.

(*d*) The Temple was to see the fulfilment of God's purposes (ver. 9). Here the essential identity of the second temple with Solomon's is affirmed, thus confirming that extensive repair rather than a new building was needed. From the building of Solomon's temple to the destruction of Herod's in A.D. 70 it was essentially the same building.

The view that the rebuilding of the Temple only began in 521 B.C. and that it was done mainly by those that had never been taken into captivity, rather than by those that had returned from Babylonia, bases itself confidently on the expression "all ye people of the land" (ver. 4). It is perfectly true that in Ezra "the people (or peoples) of the land" is a technical expression both for the other peoples living in Palestine and for those of Israelite origin who had never gone into captivity and were often semi-heathen. But since we cannot date Ezra before 400 B.C. at the earliest, it seems hardly scholarship to assume that the phrase must have had the same technical meaning more than a hundred years earlier, the more so as less than a century before that it meant simply the common people in general (II Kings 23: 30). The assumption is the more remarkable, because the term "the remnant of the people" otherwise used by Haggai (1: 12; 2: 2) is by

common consent a technical term meaning those that had
returned from captivity. The use of "all ye people of the
land" may simply be an encouragement by reminding them
that they once again possessed the land.

The Third Message (2: 10–19).

In the interval between Haggai's second and third message
another prophet, Zechariah, had arisen to stress that not
merely outward but also inward turning to God was necessary (Zech. 1: 2–6). Now on the very day that the work of
repair started Haggai came with a further message of encouragement (cf. 2: 10 with 2: 18).

It is strongly urged that since the foundation was then
laid (ver. 18) it could not have been laid sixteen years earlier
(Ezra. 3: 10f). It has already been pointed out that in any
case there was no need to lay foundations. Then the Hebrew
is far less concrete than the English translation might suggest.
The phrase could probably be legitimately translated "since
the day that Jehovah's temple was begun," the reference
being to the solemn inaugural ceremony which would have
been held equally at the recommencement of the work. Ezra
5: 16 is no contradiction. Obviously the elders of Jerusalem
would not have compromised their position with Tattenai by con-
fessing that the work had ever come to an end, which officially it
had not. They would have represented it as a slowing down.

Haggai's argument is based on a ceremonial technicality,
viz. while holiness is not contagious, uncleanness is. Therefore the presence of uncleanness more than counteracts the
presence of holiness, the dead body of the sanctuary nullifies
the effect of the altar (cf. ver. 14). "From this day will I
bless you" (ver. 19); some immediate sign is suggested. The
prophet was speaking in December, when rain was absolutely
necessary, if the seed was to be sown in time to be ready for
harvest, so the sign was probably the beginning of the rains.

The Fourth Message (2: 20–23).

With the promise to the people came also a personal
promise to Zerubbabel, who, once he had been stirred by
Haggai's call, seems to have been the driving force behind the
rebuilding. By doing this he jeopardized his official position
(cf. Ezra 5: 4). So he received a special promise of protection.
(Joshua, the high priest, had nothing to lose, everything to
gain by the rebuilding, so he is not mentioned.) Apparently
in the prophetic visions coming troubles amalgamate themselves with the final troubles of the Day of the Lord (cf. ver. 21
with 2: 6) and so Zerubbabel looks forward to Zerubbabel's
greater descendant (cf. Matt. 1: 13).

CHAPTER XV

ZECHARIAH

THE STRUCTURE OF ZECHARIAH

A. The Visions of Zechariah—Chs. 1-8.

1—Ch. 1: 1-6.   The Call to Repentance.
2—Ch. 1: 7-17.   Vision I—The Angel among the Myrtles.
3—Ch. 1: 18-21.   Vision II—Four Horns and Four Craftsmen.
4—Ch. 2: 1-13.   Vision III—The Unneeded Measuring Line.
5—Ch. 3: 1-10.   Vision IV—The Acquittal of the High Priest.
6—Ch. 4: 1-14.   Vision V—The Golden Lampstand.
7—Ch. 5: 1-4.   Vision VI—The Flying Roll.
8—Ch. 5: 5-11.   Vision VII—The Ephah.
9—Ch. 6: 1-8.   Vision VIII—The Four Chariots.
10—Ch. 6: 9-15.   The Crowning of Joshua.
11—Chs. 7, 8.   A New Era.

B. The Establishment of Messiah's Kingdom—Chs. 9-14.

1—Chs. 9, 10.   The Deliverance of Israel and Judah.
2—Ch. 11.   The Rejection of the True Shepherd.
3—Chs. 12-14.   The Final Deliverance of Jerusalem.

The Problem of Authorship.

THAT Zechariah falls clearly into two distinct parts (chs. 1-8; 9-14) is denied by none. Nor is it denied that the differences between the two parts are so great that had they stood separately in the Bible none would have thought of bringing them together. It has also been shown, though this is not universally recognized, that there is a line of division in the second part as well, viz. chs. 9-11; 12-14. With this must be connected the fact that 9: 1; 12: 1; Mal. 1: 1 all contain a formula unique in the prophetic books, viz. "the burden (or oracle) of the word of Jehovah . . ."

As early as 1653 Mede attributed chs. 9-14 to Jeremiah on the basis of Matt. 27: 9, which attributes Zech 11: 12f to that prophet. Modern widely diverging views may be roughly classified as follows:

123

(1) The whole book is by Zechariah.[1] This view is entirely tenable, but does not really explain the facts.

(2) The second part is a unity and is later than Zechariah, though there are wide variations in the date suggested.[2]

(3) Zech. 9–11; Zech. 12–14; Mal. 1–4 are three anonymous prophecies—for the authorship of Malachi see ch. XVI—of which the first is pre-exilic, the second post-exilic, but not much later than Zechariah, the third not later than 450 B.C.

(4) This is much as the preceding, but it places the two sections of Zech. 9–14 not earlier than the time of Alexander the Great (330 B.C.), some putting portions as late as Maccabean times right down to 100 B.C.[3]

We personally tend to the third view. There is no valid reason why there should not be anonymous prophetic portions in the Old Testament, and if there are, the end of the Book of the Twelve would be the natural place for them. Once Malachi was looked on as a proper name, it was almost inevitable that the other two portions should be taken up into Zechariah, the more so as this made the total of Minor Prophets twelve, the number of the tribes of Israel.

Contacts between the style of chs. 9–11 and Jeremiah are too slight to furnish any proofs on literary grounds for Mede's attribution. At the same time there is very much in these chapters than cannot find any really satisfactory explanation on the supposition of a post-exilic date. The mention of Assyria in 10 : 11 is an outstanding example. If the section is pre-exilic, it will date between the captivity of the North and the fall of Nineveh. 9 : 13 no more demands a post-exilic date than does Joel 3 : 6.

It is difficult to understand the reasoning that would attribute a really late date to Zech. 9–14. It ignores the universally recognized fact that the canon of the prophets was closed at the latest by 200 B.C. and that the LXX translation of the prophets will have been made between 200 and 150 B.C. That they were not officially included in the canon after its having been closed is certain; that they were smuggled into both the Hebrew and the LXX is a nightmare.

The Prophet and his Message.

Zechariah was the grandson of Iddo (1: 1), a priest who returned from Babylonia with Zerubbabel (Neh. 12 : 4, cf.

[1] So ISBE, article Zechariah, Book of; Young, pp. 269–273; Baron: *The Visions and Prophecies of Zechariah*, ch. XIII.

[2] So Barnes: Haggai, Zechariah and Malachi (C.B.).

[3] So HDB, article Zechariah, Book of; Driver, LOT, pp. 348–355; Kirkpatrick, pp. 442–456; for the extreme view Oesterley and Robinson: *An Introduction to the Books of the Old Testament*, pp. 419–425.

12: 16). The non-mention of his father Berechiah in Neh. 12: 16; Ezra 5: 1; 6: 14 suggests that he may have died young. Nothing more is known or can be inferred from his prophecies about Zechariah, except that he was evidently a student of his prophetic predecessors. The suggestion on the basis of 2: 4 that he was young depends on what is almost certainly a false interpretation.

Chs. 1–8 present many difficulties in interpretation mainly because of the apocalyptic visions they contain (see p. 115) in which the prophet's own time and the final crisis of the Day of the Lord tend to become blended.

Chs. 9–14 are also apocalyptic, but in the general style of the older apocalyptic passages. The background and some-times even the foreground are vague, and exact interpretation is at times impossible. The difficulty is increased by the chapters consisting of a considerable number of non-connected shorter prophecies bound together merely by an inner spiritual link.

Just as in Ezek. 40–48 God does not appear, and in the visions He does not speak directly to Zechariah. His place is taken by that mysterious figure from the earlier books of the Old Testament, the Angel of Jehovah. In numerous passages the angel of Jehovah means no more than the angel, any angel, already introduced. In such cases the context makes it clear, and this is true of the only passage where the term is used of a man (Mal. 2: 7, q.v.); for Hag. 1: 13 see p. 120f. But in other passages the context demands that the Angel of Jehovah should be an exalted and unique figure. Davidson defines Him excellently, "The Angel of the Lord is Jehovah present in definite time and particular place."[1] The tra-ditional Christian interpretation of the Angel of Jehovah as the preincarnate Son is, we believe, correct, but this is based on general analogies rather than on any definite Scriptural proof. The use of the term in Zechariah stresses that though God is transcendent, far above His creation, yet He finds means of keeping in touch with His own people, and that personally and not through some mere angelic intermediary.

In the former section of the book the transcendent power of God is particularly stressed by the constant use of Jehovah of hosts (*Jehovah Zeba'oth*). In these eight chapters, if we omit a couple of cases where Jehovah means the Angel of Jehovah, we have Jehovah of hosts used 48 times, Jehovah only 33. This is unique in the Old Testament, the nearest comparable case being Haggai (—there is nothing comparable in chs. 9–14, where the figures are 8 and 39, surely a very strong argument against authorship by Zechariah of these chapters).

[1] *The Theology of the Old Testament*, p. 297f.

Whether the name Jehovah of hosts may have meant merely Jehovah of the armies of Israel, when we first find it used at the end of the period of the Judges (cf. I Sam. 1: 3), we cannot know for certain, though we doubt it. In the mouth of the great prophets the hosts are the hosts of heaven, and that is the meaning for Zechariah too. With him it has an even deeper meaning, for in exile the Jews had become familiar with the Babylonian worship of the heavenly bodies and later with the new Iranian teaching of Zoroaster with its concept of hosts of warring angels. Zechariah affirms that Jehovah is the God of whatever powers and hosts there may be. The LXX has understood his meaning very well. Normally it simply transliterates *Zeba'oth* as *Sebaoth*, but in Zechariah it renders *Pantokrator*, All-Sovereign.

Though the object of the first eight chapters is to encourage the builders of the Temple in their difficulties, the message is shot through with that deep moral earnestness that is never far distant from the true prophets; it also looks forward all the time to the Day of the Lord.

The Call to Repentance (1: 1–6).

This opening section strikes the underlying assumption behind all the future encouragement. God will bless, but only a people that have returned to Him and that do His will. Zechariah reinforces his appeal by recalling the past.

The Eight Visions (1: 7–6: 8).

While there is an undoubted predictive element in these visions, they are not really comparable with those in Daniel. Efforts to see in them mainly the more distant future of the Jews are hardly convincing. This is equally true of the attempt to interpret them solely as a symbolic description of Zechariah's own time and the immediate future. A major element in them is timeless, stressing major spiritual truths in the light of the prophet's own time.

The first and last vision with their message of divine sovereignty provide the framework for the rest. They divide naturally into three groups: visions I to III are concerned mainly with the rebuilding of the Temple, IV and V with Joshua and Zerubbabel, the leaders of the people, VI to VIII with the spiritual transformation of the people.

I.   The Angel among the Myrtles (1: 7–17).

In a night vision Zechariah sees a man, later identified as the Angel of Jehovah, sitting on His horse "among the myrtle trees that were in the bottom." He had just been joined by other angelic riders belonging to three distinct groups as

shown by the colour of their horses; they give a report on the
earth that all was still and at rest (ver. 11). The Angel of
Jehovah then pleads for Jerusalem and there comes a com-
fortable message for the prophet (vers. 14–17).

Taken literally ver. 11 cannot be true of the second year of
Darius. Even if, as we think, the two main rebellions had
been broken, there was obviously still fighting to come. On
the other hand the 70 years of ver. 12 (a round figure probably
based on Jer. 25: 11; 29: 10 for it was about 66 years since
the destruction of the Temple) tie down the vision to the
prophet's own time. The clue is given by ver. 15, for the same
people must be meant as in ver. 11, and the mere fact of peace
would not have awakened God's displeasure.

The Angel of Jehovah has come to Jerusalem, but not into
it, for the Temple has not yet been rebuilt. "The bottom"
is somewhere near the city, and is probably chosen for the
scene of the vision, even as is the Hebrew word that describes
it, to typify the low position of the Jews. The angel riders had
ridden out in three directions (west of Palestine is the Mediterranean!) and now give their report. When it is realized that
they are not being sent out, but that their task is finished, it
will prevent any linking of this vision with 6: 1–8, with Daniel
or Revelation. All the peoples were at arrogant ease and self-
confident peace with no thought of Jehovah of hosts or of the
state of His people. It is here that we find the timelessness of
the vision. The colours of the horses only distinguish the
three groups and have no further meaning.

II. Four Horns and Four Craftsmen (1: 18–21).

How God is to carry out His purposes is shown in the next
vision. Out of the surrounding night (ver. 8) Zechariah sees
four great threatening horns. They are not identified, and
to do so with the four beasts of Dan. 7 or otherwise is entirely
to miss the point. There are four for the four corners of the
earth, and they represent all who have oppressed and scattered
Israel and Judah, or who ever will.

Equally unidentified are the four craftsmen (both A.V.
carpenters, R.V. smiths are too precise) who frighten them
away—fray (ver. 21) is too weak. God has His remedy for
every oppressor. But the fact that they are craftsmen almost
certainly points to the rebuilding of the Temple, which would
be the best way of guaranteeing the divine help.

III. The Unneeded Measuring Line (Ch. 2).

Zechariah sees a young man—not an angel—going out to
measure the proposed line of Jerusalem's walls. Then the
interpreting angel (1: 9, 19) went forth, i.e. appeared (ver. 3)

and commanded yet "another angel" to run and stop the young man, for his work was unnecessary. The reason was not so much that Jerusalem would be larger than any man's optimism (ver. 4) but rather that Jehovah Himself would be their wall (ver. 5).

This ends the first group of visions and so there follows a call to those still in exile to return (vers. 6–9) and a picture of Zion's future glory. Though ver. 13 could refer to Jehovah's intervention in Zechariah's day, it obviously looks forward to the Day of the Lord.

IV.   The Acquittal of the High Priest (Ch. 3).

There is no suggestion here that the scene is set in heaven. Perhaps the most striking feature is Joshua's complete passivity. The reason probably lies in the ambiguity of "stand before" (ver. 1), which makes us misinterpret the vision. The phrase may mean to stand in attendance (ver. 4), or to stand before a judge, but it also means to carry out one's priestly ministry, e.g. Deut. 10: 8, and that is its probable meaning here.

Zechariah sees Joshua standing ministering, perhaps in the rebuilt Temple, for it is a vision. All unknown to him Satan is standing ready to accuse him as the prosecutor—there is no indication that he had already spoken. There is no suggestion of personal fault on Joshua's part. His priestly garments are filthy because he represents the people. Consistently with that there is no personal confession.

Here Zechariah strikes the deeper note suggested by his introductory prophecy. The acceptance of Joshua and so of the people is an act of pure grace which looks to a yet future act of God (ver. 9). That God is willing to acknowledge Joshua and his fellow priests is a sign (ver. 8, R.V.) of the future removal of sin, which is linked with the Messiah, the Shoot (R.V. mg , cf. 6: 12 mg.; Isa. 4: 2 mg.; 11: 1; Jer. 23: 5 mg.; 33: 15). The interpretation of ver. 9 is very difficult, but there is no real doubt that the stone is that of 4: 7, and that it is to be linked with Ps. 118: 22; Isa. 28: 16. It is a headstone, i.e. the last stone to be put in place, but it will not fit unless the building has been made exactly to plan; it has been carved by Jehovah Himself.

V.   The Golden Lampstand (Ch. 4).

The vision is of a seven-branched lampstand, which differed from that in the Temple by having a bowl above the lamps, supplying oil to the lamps by seven golden tubes. This means that providing the bowl was kept filled with oil, the lights were not dependent on human care as was the case in the

Temple. At first sight it would appear that the two olive trees (vers. 3, 12) supplied the necessary oil to the bowl. But the difficult Hebrew of ver. 12 may and probably does mean that the oil is being emptied out of the bowl not merely into the lamps but into the olive trees as well; the trees are obviously Zerubbabel and Joshua. If this is correct, it means that in the theocracy the light of witness is not maintained by the civil and religious administration, but they and the light are maintained by God. It would seem that ver. 10b (read, These seven are the eyes of Jehovah . . .) is the answer to ver. 5. For the idea of the seven eyes cf. 3: 9; Rev. 1: 4.

Just as the previous vision contained a message to Joshua looking forward to the Messiah, so here is a similar message to Zerubbabel (vers. 6–10a). Though it promises that Zerubbabel will finish building the Temple, it looks to Zerubbabel's Messianic descendant, for the headstone is both Messianic and indeed the Messiah (see above).

VI. *The Flying Roll* (5: 1–4).

Zechariah sees a great sheet of leather 30′ by 15′ (the roll was unrolled!) flying through the air. Since these are the dimensions of the Holy Place in the Tabernacle, it is reasonable to suppose that the roll contained the main provisions of the Law. Whenever in the vision it came to the house of the thief and perjurer—typical sinners—it brought destruction with it. The promise had been given in 3: 9 of the removal of sin. Here we are reminded that where men do not repent, the removal of sin implies the destruction of the sinner.

VII. *The Ephah* (5: 5–11).

Though the vision clearly shows the removal of wickedness from the land after the individual sinners had been dealt with, there seems no measure of agreement as to how its details should be interpreted. This has opened the door to various imaginative efforts that do not call for mention. The ephah and the talent may suggest that commerce is envisaged; it is quite possible that the woman personifies idolatry. In any case we have a promise which obviously looks to the Day of the Lord for its perfect fulfilment.

VIII. *The Four Chariots* (6: 1–8).

The visions end as they begin with the sovereignty of God over the earth. The four winds (or spirits) of heaven issue out between the mountains of brass (probably the popular idea of the gate of heaven) in form as chariots, which imply war. The colour of the horses probably merely serves to distinguish them one from another and has no further meaning

I

(cf. 1: 8). Any linking with Daniel is far-fetched, and while some particular situation in the prophet's own time is doubtless envisaged, the general certainty of God's rule is the fundamental thought.

The Crowning of Joshua (6: 9–15).

There is an inner contradiction in this incident, for to crown the high priest as Messianic king (ver. 12f) would be to run counter to all prophecy. In addition the promise that he should build the Temple had been earlier given to Zerubbabel (4: 9). As a result most moderns assume that it was Zerubbabel that was crowned, but when the Persians heard of it he lost his position and perhaps his life. To hide the disappointment the prophecy was distorted by substituting Joshua's name. The plausibility of this view is increased by the mistaken English translation in ver. 12, "Behold the man . . .''; it should be "Behold a man . . .", not necessarily identifying the person crowned with the prophecy.

Note that we are not dealing with a crowning or anointing ceremony. The crown (the singular is correct, see mg. to vers. 11, 14) is a sign of honour rather than royalty—the Hebrew does not use the usual word for the royal crown. At the same time it was an honour which might indeed have been fatal for Zerubbabel, but not for Joshua. Zechariah gives honour to Joshua, but indicates that Zerubbabel ranks higher for he is the ancestor of the Messiah. In so doing, however, he foreshadows him who was to be priest-king for ever after the order of Melchizedek (Ps. 110: 4; Heb. 6: 20).

While like Haggai, Zechariah saw in Zerubbabel the foreshadowing of the Messiah (see note on Hag. 2: 23), he did not think him the Messiah. The language always falls short of complete identification. In addition there is always an eschatological element present which reminds us that Zechariah is looking to the future, however near he may hope it to be. It may be for this reason that he prefers to use the title Shoot, which although it has Messianic connotations cannot be said to be purely Messianic.

We do not doubt that the R.V. mg. is correct in ver. 13 and that it is a promise that Joshua shall share in Zerubbabel's rule; at the same time the Hebrew is ambiguous, and in its deeper fulfilment it points to Jesus Christ the priest-king as expressed by the R.V. text.

The New Era (Chs. 7, 8).

The fall of Jerusalem had led to the introduction of four fasts (8: 19)—for that of the fourth month see II Kings 25: 3f; Jer. 39: 2f; for that of the fifth II Kings 25: 8ff; Jer. 52: 12ff;

for that of the seventh II Kings 25: 25; for that of the tenth II Kings 25: 1; Jer. 39: 1. The men of Bethel had now come to realize that with the restoration the keeping of them was questionable sense—ritual often paralyses common sense and is maintained long after it has lost its meaning—and so they came to lay the matter before the Jerusalem authorities. This led to a series of four prophetic messages by Zechariah.

7: 4–14 deals with the true meaning of fasting and reminds us strongly of Isa. 58: 1–12; it reaffirms the old prophetic stress on social righteousness.

8: 1–8 gives a picture of the glorious future of Jerusalem.

8: 9–17 contrasts the condition after the return from exile with the future, and gives the conditions for prosperity.

8: 18–23 gives a concluding picture of the future when Jerusalem will be the religious centre of the world.

The Establishment of Messiah's Kingdom (Chs. 9–14).

We have already pointed out that these chapters are apocalyptic, and as is usual in such prophecies the general drift is clear enough, but detailed interpretation is impossible —he who thinks otherwise should learn humility from those as good as he who have interpreted them otherwise. We must content ourselves with pointing out the main subdivisions.

(a) 9: 1–8. Jehovah's vengeance on Israel's neighbours.

(b) 9: 9f. The Messianic king of peace.

(c) 9: 11–17. Israel freed from captivity is victorious over her enemies. Obviously the fulfilment of this must precede (b) unless it is completely spiritualized.

(d) 10: 1f. A warning against superstition and magic arts. It may be in its present position because the closing words link it superficially with what follows.

(e) 10: 3–12. The raising up of rulers by God who shall lead Judah and Ephraim back to the land. Though not exclusively Messianic, there is a Messianic note in it. For the use of shepherd see p. 111.

(f) 11: 1ff. A visitation on the land. There is no possibility of identifying the particular invader. Since the mention of shepherds may explain its position here, we cannot even assume that it is eschatological.

(g) 11: 4–14. The rejection of Jehovah's Shepherd. The passage becomes easier when one remembers that the prophet is acting allegorically (with an imaginary flock?), and sometimes it is the prophet, sometimes God, who speaks in the first person.

(h) 11: 15ff. The appointment of a worthless king as a punishment. Probably a historic figure of the past used to prefigure one yet future.

(*i*) 12: 1–9. The deliverance of Jerusalem, cf. 14: 1–15.

(*j*) 12: 10–14. Judah's repentance. On the basis of John 19: 37; Rev. 1: 7, it is probably better to follow the R.V. mg. in ver. 10. The reference in ver. 11 has never been satisfactorily explained.

(*k*) 13: 1–6. The cleansing of Judah from all taint of sin and false prophecy.

(*l*) 13: 7ff. The smiting of the Shepherd, and its fruit. Some link this with 11: 15ff, but there is really no serious ground for this. It is far more satisfactory to link in with 12 : 10 and refer it to our Lord. The Shepherd is called Jehovah's fellow, because Jehovah is the supreme Shepherd of Israel, cf. I Pet. 5: 1ff.

(*m*) 14: 1–5. The Lord comes to deliver Jerusalem.

(*n*) 14: 6–21. Millennial glory. Read the mg. in ver. 21.

CHAPTER XVI

MALACHI

THE STRUCTURE OF MALACHI

"I HAVE LOVED YOU"

A. The Proof of God's Love—Ch. 1: 1-5.

B. Obstacles to the Enjoyment of God's Love—Ch. 1: 6-3: 12.
    1—Chs. 1: 6-2: 9. Lack of Respect and Reverence towards God.
        (a) Ch. 1: 6-14. By the People.
        (b) Ch. 2: 1-9. By the Priests.
    2—Ch. 2: 10-16. Inhumanity and Apostasy.
    3—Chs. 2: 17-3: 6. Despising of God's Promises and Commandments.
    4—Ch. 3: 7-12. Withholding of Tithes.

C. God's Loving Protection of the Pious in the Day of Judgment—Chs. 3: 13-4: 3.

D. The Final call to Repentance—Ch. 4: 4-6.

The Prophet and His Message.

MALACHI means "My Messenger" or "My Angel," or if it is abbreviated, as is just possible, "The Messenger of Jehovah." Either is a highly improbable name to give to a child. We shall be almost certainly correct in regarding the book as anonymous, and Malachi as a title which the prophet gave himself, perhaps because he deliberately wished to efface himself.[1] Not merely a great reformer like Calvin, but most of the Church Fathers, including Jerome, many of the early rabbis, the Targum (the official Jewish translation into Aramaic) and the LXX (second century B.C.; though not the later added heading) all fail to see a proper name here and regard the book as anonymous. In addition the New Testament never quotes him by name. On the other hand there have been those from at least the second century A.D. who have looked on Malachi as a proper name. We have no hesitation in following the vast majority of modern scholars in regarding the book as anonymous.[2]

It is obvious that Malachi is later than Haggai and Zechariah, for the Temple has been rebuilt. He is hardly likely to

[1] See HDB and ISBE, article Malachi.

[2] Exceptions are Pusey: *The Minor Prophets VI*, p. 167, who thinks, "It may be that he framed it for himself" (*sic!*), and Young, p. 275f.

be later than Nehemiah, for the sins that he rebukes are just those that Nehemiah had to deal with. Pusey looks on him as contemporaneous, "Yet he probably bore a great part in the reformation, in which Nehemiah co-operated outwardly . . ."[1] This hardly fits in with the general impression created by Nehemiah. Others place him in the interval between Nehemiah's two governorships, but this presupposes an immediate slump in the behaviour of the people which again is hardly suggested by Nehemiah. On the other hand there are problems connected with the activity of Ezra and Nehemiah which would keep us from all dogmatism. Personally we prefer a date not much before 450 B.C., shortly before the reforms were begun.

Beyond the fact that he probably moved in the Temple circles there is nothing that we can infer about "Malachi" personally. His book is entirely in prose and carefully and skilfully put together.

His message concerns God's love. In the difficulties of the post-exilic community, which were so contrary to the high hopes with which they had returned, and which had decreased but little after the rebuilding of the Temple, in spite of the glowing promises of Haggai and Zechariah, it was easy to doubt the love of God. "Malachi" is concerned to show that there is proof of God's love, that the enjoyment of that love was being hindered by the sins of the people, and how the love would reveal itself in the future.

The Proof of God's Love (1: 2–5).

The supreme proof of God's love to the Jew was His choice of Jacob in grace. "Malachi" points out that the same principle was operating in his own day, for even if the Jew was weak, Edom was weaker still. For the situation mirrored here see p. 96.

"But Esau I hated" (ver. 3)—as Snaith has pointed out[2] the love of God in the Old Testament is, above all, election love. Since in old Hebrew there were no intermediate shades, not to elect, not to love, was to hate.

Obstacles to the Enjoyment of God's Love (1: 6–3: 12).

The love of God, which made Israel His firstborn (Exod. 4: 22), expected respect and reverence from His children. Where these did not exist, the love of God could not be experienced. This wrong attitude of the people was shown in five different ways.

(1) There was the gross disrespect shown to Jehovah (1: 6–14) by bringing Him sacrifices without heart-respect (ver. 7), of a quality unworthy of the Persian governor's table

[1] Pusey, *op. cit.*, p. 169.

[2] *The Distinctive Ideas of the Old Testament*, ch. VI.

(ver. 8), and by treating the whole matter as indifferent and a burden (ver. 12f); some even descended to gross deceit (ver. 14). Far better no sacrifices at all (ver. 10). Though the priests are specially addressed, for it was they as guardians of the altar who made such behaviour possible, it is clear that we are dealing with a widespread attitude among the people.

This was the worse because of the growing respect with which Jehovah was being regarded wherever the dispersion extended (ver. 11). This famous verse is interpreted along three lines.

(a) The A.V. in common with most of the early Church Fathers and those moderns who tend to be traditionalists look upon it as a prophecy of the spread of Christianity. Linguistically this is entirely possible, but it does not do justice to the context.

(b) Some moderns, specially among the more liberal, take it to mean that Jehovah accepts all true and sincere worship and sacrifice as though it had been knowingly addressed to Him. This would suit a treatise on comparative religion better than an exposition of the Old Testament and cannot fairly be extracted from the prophet's language.

(c) The most likely interpretation—which does not rule out (a) as a deeper fulfilment—is that the dispersion, which even then was more zealous than those who had returned, cf. the work of Ezra and Nehemiah, was making the name and worship of Jehovah widely known. Since incense symbolizes prayer, and the offering is the *minchah*, the meal or gift offering, which could metaphorically be applied to all gifts to God, no actual Temple sacrifices need be envisaged.

(2) The priests are then specially arraigned (2: 1-9) for their neglect of their special privileges as teachers of the Law (vers. 7ff). So high do they stand in God's economy that the priest is called the angel of Jehovah of hosts (ver. 7—A.V., R.V. messenger; the context prevents any misunderstanding). We can see that we are in the twilight of prophecy, for the priest is now to stand alone as the expounder of the already revealed will of God. It should be noticed that the stress is not on sacrificing, which spiritually was not the chief priestly task, cf. Deut. 33: 8ff, where it is mentioned last.

(3) The inhumanity of the people (2: 10-16), which was a contradiction of God's love, was specially shown in the divorce of their wives, and this became apostacy by their subsequent marriage with heathen women (ver. 11). "Malachi" is not seeking to set aside the regulations of Deut. 24: 1-4 about divorce, but their enforcement in their true spiritual sense. The phrase "wife of thy youth" suggests a marriage of long standing; if there had been anything to justify divorce, it would have shown itself much earlier; in addition after these

years it would be very difficult for her to find another husband.
These divorces were just treachery. Since no woman was
allowed to come to the altar, ver. 18 is a powerful metaphorical
expression.

The Old Testament obviously looks on monogamy as the
ideal, and we do not get the impression from it that divorce
was common; the better elements in Jewry were always
against it. The famous dictum in the Mishnah, "And the
School of Hillel say: [He may divorce her] even if she spoiled
a dish for him, for it is written, Because he hath found in her
indecency in *anything*. R. Akiba says: Even if he found
another fairer than she, for it is written, And it shall be if she
finds no favour in his eyes . . ."[1] is a legal argument. These
men did not act according to their argument, nor would they
have encouraged others so to act.

(4) There was disbelief in the reality of Jehovah's promises
and threats and much open sin (2: 17–3: 6). The former reminds
us of Zeph. 1: 12. These will be dealt with by the coming of
the Angel of the covenant (3: 2. R.V. mg.), *i.e.* the Angel
of Jehovah, in the judgment of the Day of the Lord. The
promise that closes this section (3: 6) may seem out of place
until we remember that even the judgment of God is a sign
of His love and an accomplishing of His purpose. It was the
sinners that would be burnt out, not the whole people.

(5) Finally the people were withholding His dues from God
(3: 7–12). There can be no question of the prophet's trying
to bribe the people (ver. 10ff). It is prophetic logic that if the
barrier to the enjoyment of God's love is removed, the gifts
of His love will be enjoyed as well.

God's Loving Protection of the Pious in the Day of Judgment
(3: 13–4: 3).

Since the disloyal element in the people exists and persists (3: 13ff), there must be judgment. But the loyal have
been noted (3: 16) and in the day of judgment they will be
preserved (3: 17), so that the difference between the two
parties will be clearly seen. The result of judgment will be
the triumph of the righteous (4: 2f).

The Final Call to Repentance (4: 4ff).

A fitting end to the prophetic books. It looks back to the
revelation of God on which the whole prophetic message is based
and forward to the fulfilment of all the prophetic hopes. It offers
the choice of repentance (ver. 6, see R.V. mg.) or the ban. In
the Synagogue ver. 5 is read a second time after ver. 6 to avoid
ending with the ban, cf. Isa. 66: 23f, p. 62, but it is only Jesus
Christ, the fulfilment of the prophets, who can raise the ban.

[1] *Gittin*, ix, 10.

CHAPTER XVII

DANIEL

THE STRUCTURE OF DANIEL

A. The Present—Chs. 1-6.
    1—Ch. 1. God the Protector of the captives.
    2—Ch. 2. God the Revealer of the future.
    3—Ch. 3. God the Lord of fire.
    4—Ch. 4. God the Humbler of the proud.
    5—Ch. 5. God the Avenger of His honour.
    6—Ch. 6. God the Tamer of beasts.

B. The Future—Chs. 7-12.
    1—Ch. 7. The End of World History.
    2—Ch. 8. The Enemy of the Saints.
    3—Ch. 9. The Messiah the Prince.
    4—Chs. 10-12. The Fortunes of Israel.

WE deal with Daniel last, not because we consider that this is its true chronological position, but because both the Hebrew canon of Scripture and the nature of its contents put it outside the Prophets in the strict sense of the word.

Daniel, with its stress on the sovereignty of God, which not only compels rebellious men to do His will, but that even at the very moment of His appointing, has always been the most obnoxious of Old Testament books to the humanist, and a chief centre of his attacks. To complicate matters, the book seems to invite attack and to make the task of the critic the easier. For over half a century now the overwhelming majority of Old Testament scholars have taken the non-historical nature of Daniel for granted.

The results have been disastrous, for both sides have come to the study of the difficulties and the exegesis of the book with such bias that they are seldom able to do it justice.

"Historical Errors."

Except incidentally we shall not refer to the allegedly unhistorical statements in the book. Those who are interested are referred to the works mentioned in the bibliography. These arguments are not nearly so important as often imagined, for the modern scholar has seriously weakened the force of his own attack.

Though scholars differ in details, virtually all who reject the traditional authorship are agreed that the book *in its present form* was produced about 168 B.C.[1] The writer attributed his visions to Daniel to get his message, in whose truth he profoundly believed, more readily accepted. Charles puts it thus: "How then from the third century B.C. onward was the man to act who felt himself charged with a real message of God to his day and generation? The tyranny of the Law and the petrified orthodoxies of his time, compelled him to resort to pseudonymity. And if these grounds had in themselves been insufficient for the adoption of pseudonymity, there was the further ground—the formation of the Canon. When once the prophetic Canon was closed, no book of a prophetic character could gain canonization as such, nor could it gain a place among the sacred writings at all unless its date was believed to be as early as Ezra."[2]

It should be clear that such a pious imposture could never have succeeded, if the new book had contradicted the already existing Scripture. Now, with only one major exception, the main "historical errors" are contradictions of Scripture as well. Thus the modern view virtually answers its own difficulties. Were the book a second-century production, we may guarantee that the writer must have had fully adequate grounds for his apparent contradictions of other Scriptures. The bigger the problem, *e.g.* the identity of Darius the Mede, the surer we may be that there is an adequate explanation. But the same argument holds if the book is dated earlier. Fiction that hopes to be accepted as history must be meticulous in its accuracy; how much more if it wishes to be accepted as inspired as well.

There is a tendency to underrate the critical acumen of the period. The Talmud shows us that the early rabbis were very conscious of discrepancies, real or apparent, in the Scriptures. We may not agree with the means by which they explained them away, but that does not diminish the clear-sightedness by which they saw them.

In all fairness it must be added that this only meets the charge of specific error, not that of giving a generally false picture of the times described. This is a charge more easily made than proved. Since, however, there is an increasing tendency to attribute the narrative part of Daniel to the fifth century B.C., it should be clear that the charge is not a serious one.

---

[1] For the usual modern view see HDB, article Daniel, Book of; Driver, LOT, ch. XI. Against see ISBE, article Daniel, Book of; Young, ch. XXIV; Lattey: *The Book of Daniel* and the Bibliography.

[2] Daniel (The Century Bible), p. xvi.

The Linguistic Problem.

Driver's dictum is well known: "The *Persian* words pre-suppose a period after the Persian empire had been well established: the Greek words *demand*, the Hebrew *supports*, and the Aramaic *permits* a date *after the conquest of Palestine by Alexander the Great* (332 B.C.)."[1] We are not going to enter into linguistic discussions here, for while it has been proved that the language is compatible with the book's having been written in the fifth century B.C., nothing more than the bare possibility of a sixth-century date can be shown.

But the linguistic phenomena are more complex than the dictum just quoted suggests. From 2: 4b ("O king, live for ever . . .") to 7: 28 the book is not written in Hebrew but in Aramaic, and it is almost universally recognized that the words "in the Syrian language" in 2: 4 do not mean that Daniel spoke in that language—for Babylonian was the court language—but are merely a warning to the copyist that the language is changing. This change of language sets a problem that has seldom been adequately considered by conservatives.

The usual explanation that Aramaic, an international language, is used because these chapters deal with the nations, while chs. 8–12 deal with the Jews, will hardly hold water. 8: 26; 12: 4, 9 seem to preclude any idea that the book was to be widely circulated. In any case, we should expect under this theory the Aramaic to begin with 2: 1 or even 1: 1.

Many suggestions have been made by scholars, but there is only one which we consider covers all aspects of the problem. It is that the book was translated into Aramaic a century or more after its original composition. In course of time part of the original Hebrew was lost, and it was replaced by the Aramaic. The objection that the break could not have come so conveniently seems to have little force. It might have been anywhere in ch. 2, but the scribe responsible for the present form of Daniel would have made the transfer at what seemed the most suitable spot.

It can hardly be just a coincidence that all the Greek words, and all but three of the Persian, are in the Aramaic section. If the writer were a catcher up of foreign words, one would expect a more even distribution of them. If, however, the Aramaic is a century or two later, there is no difficulty in the translator's use of words which had become far commoner by his time. It will, however, be objected that any such loss of the Hebrew is inconceivable; but what evidence there is hardly supports the objection.

[1] Driver, LOT, p. 508.

When did Daniel enter the Canon?

Most Christians (and Jews) take their Bibles for granted, and never ask themselves how the various books came to be recognized as inspired. The history of the New Testament canon shows that while certain books were recognized as inspired within a generation of their having been written, others were regarded with suspicion for a considerable period of time. We have similar evidence for the Old Testament, for as late as the end of the first century A.D. and possibly even later, the right of certain books to be in the Canon was being challenged.

Great stress is laid by the opponents of Daniel's authorship on the fact that the book is not certainly referred to or quoted before 140 B.C. The argument from silence is always dangerous, and here the more so because we have so little literature from this period. For all that, it should not be dismissed offhand. The book is unique in the Old Testament; the form of vision, though prepared for by Ezekiel, is unique; the visions must have been until fairly late in the Greek period almost unintelligible; in addition, Daniel never had the standing of a prophet, and will not have seen his first vision until he was at least sixty-five. All this makes an immediate admission to the Canon improbable. In fact, everything points to the remarkable verification of certain parts of the book in the time of Antiochus Epiphanes (175–164 B.C.) as the proximate cause of its being recognized as inspired.

That Daniel circulated in inferior MSS. is shown by the LXX translation (usually dated *c.* 140 B.C., but quite possibly earlier). Not only are there many striking variants, especially in chs. 4–6, but there are three additions (to be found in the Apocrypha) running to 174 verses. It seems incredible that any such additions and variations should have entered after the book had been recognized as canonical.

In the light of these facts, there seems little ground for objecting to the possibility of the Hebrew having been replaced by Aramaic. This would sweep away the cogency of the linguistic objection, the more so as the Hebrew does not really suit a second-century date, and is not inconsistent with Daniel's position; he probably seldom spoke Hebrew after the time when he was taken captive as a lad. This is amply adequate to explain many of its peculiarities.

The Miraculous Element.

When all is said and done, the real objection to Daniel is its miraculous element, both in its histories and in its veiled but detailed foretelling of the future. The predictive element can only be removed from Daniel by doing violence to its natural meaning. The miraculous element in the histories does not pass the bounds of the credible, and in common with all Bible miracle stands or falls with the resurrection of our Lord, the greatest miracle of all.

The Christian should never forget that the narratives of Daniel receive their endorsement in Heb. 11: 33f, while the predictive truth of the visions is confirmed by our Lord Himself (Matt. 24: 15, cf. Mark 13: 14). This word of our Lord is a guarantee that the visions of chs. 9 and 10–12, in which the abomination of desolation is found, cannot be restricted to the time of Antiochus Epiphanes.

The Moral Problem.

It is the New Testament endorsement of Daniel that is really fatal to the modern view. Unfortunately the achieving of good ends by wrong means has never been rare in religious circles; but the end never does justify the means. If Daniel is a second-century work, whatever the motives of the author, it is a sham and a forgery, and we are seriously asked to believe that our Lord had not sufficient spiritual insight to recognize it as such. The period 150 B.C.—A.D. 100 did produce a large crop of pseudepigraphic works,[1] of which Enoch and II Esdras (the latter in the Apocrypha) are perhaps the best known. There is no evidence known to us that the ascriptions of authorship in these books were taken very seriously by any of the Jewish religious leaders, and yet our Lord Jesus Himself (to say nothing of all the others) was completely deceived by Daniel!

To make matters worse, according to this view He took a book which had only been intended by its author to refer to the time of Antiochus Epiphanes, and so misunderstood it, that He made it apply to things yet future!

To sum up: Over a century of controversy and study has proved inconclusive. The honest verdict on the intellectual arguments of both conservative and liberal must be, Not Proven. Here, as so often in the Bible, the final answer must be one of faith. Pusey's words are as valid to-day as when they were first written in 1864, "The book of Daniel is . . . either divine or an imposture."[2] It is in our Lord's attitude, rather than in linguistic studies and archaeological research, however valuable and commendable they may be, that we shall find the answer to the problem.

[1] These were mostly apocalyptic and eschatological works attributed to various worthies of the past.

[2] Pusey: *Daniel the Prophet*, p. 1.

Daniel the Man.

If not of royal blood, Daniel belonged to one of the best families of Judah (1: 3). After Nebuchadnezzar's victory in 605 B.C. at Carchemish, Jehoiakim had to become a vassal of Babylon (this was Jehoiakim's fourth year according to the Jewish, but third according to the Babylonian style of reckoning, 1: 1). Nebuchadnezzar carried off children of the best families, probably as hostages, Daniel among them. The story creates the impression that he will have been about fourteen.

It seems likely that Daniel was made a eunuch (see 1: 3, and much early Jewish tradition). He rapidly rose to high office (2: 48f), which he probably retained until the death of the king (562 B.C.). The impression created by ch. 5 is that he then was either retired—he will have been nearly sixty—or moved to a subordinate post, the former being the more likely. When Cyrus conquered Babylon (539 B.C.) Daniel was an old man of over eighty, and it is easy to see why his work in the reorganization of the kingdom (ch. 6) probably lasted only a year (1: 21). The last recorded date in his life is two years later (10: 1), and it is probable he died not long after. It is too little realized that it was a white-haired old man who was thrown to the lions. Daniel's age is sufficient explanation of his not returning to Palestine.

Apart from legends of no value, we have no knowledge of Daniel apart from his book. The man mentioned by Ezekiel (14: 14, 20; 28: 3) is a figure of hoar antiquity, probably mentioned in tablets discovered at Ras Shamra, dating from before 1400 B.C. His name is spelled *Dani'el* (or more likely *Dan'el*), while the hero of our book spells his *Daniyye'l*, and this is true also of two other persons of the same name, I Chron. 3: 1 and Ezra 8: 2 (Neh. 10: 6). A spelling error by Ezekiel is hardly credible.

We have not even the outline of an autobiography. The stories of Daniel and his friends are told us to reveal the sovereign power of God in action, so that we may the more readily believe the all-sovereignty of God over the future. Not Daniel and his friends, but the sovereign power of God is the topic of each story (cf. especially 2: 47; 3: 28f; 4: 2, 3, 37; 6: 25ff).

The Stories of Daniel.

Once the real purpose of the narratives in Daniel has been grasped, only a few comments on details are needed.

In the ancient world it was quite usual to honour one's god by giving him part of one's food, specially meat and wine (cf.

I Cor. 8; 10: 19–33; also Lev. 2 and 17: 3–9, this latter abrogated at least in part by Deut. 12: 15, 20f). As Nebuchadnezzar was a very religious man, it could be taken for granted that any food that came from his table had been so dedicated. There would have been little or no harm in Daniel and his friends eating this food, but to refuse to do so was one of the few acts of loyalty to Jehovah left open to them (ch. 1).

It is rather naïve to think that Nebuchadnezzar had really forgotten his dream (2: 5). He was so impressed by it that he did not want some spur-of-the-moment priestly explanation fobbed off on him. He argued shrewdly that anyone able to tell him his dream would know the explanation as well. The explanation of the dream is dealt with under the visions.

There is no justification for supposing that the golden (*i.e.* gold covered) image (3: 1) was of Nebuchadnezzar himself. It will have been of Merodach or Marduk, his favourite god. The absence of Daniel need cause no surprise, for the language of 3: 2f must not be stressed. In an empire where it might need months to reach the capital, it would never be possible to gather *all* the high functionaries of state together in one place at the same time. Provincial rule and international relationships had to be continued. The R.V. is correct in its rendering of 3: 25, "like a son of the gods"—the king was a pagan polytheist.

The LXX bears witness to considerable textual doubt in ch. 4. This may be the explanation for the change from the first to the third person in vers. 19–33. The first person would have been expected throughout.

The versions, and indeed Daniel's own explanation, create an element of doubt as to the exact form of the words written on the wall (5: 25); (a) was *Mene* written once or twice? (b) was it *Peres* (sing.) or *Parsin* (plu.—*u* equals "and")? In any case, the doubt affects neither their meaning nor the interpretation of the scene. It seems likely that the words were written in Aramaic (or more probably Hebrew—see above) and that the more educated present had no difficulty in deciphering the letters; owing to the absence of vowels (as normally the case in Semitic writing) they will have read the words: a mina, a shekel, and a half mina (or half minas, or two half minas), which made little sense. (A mina was 60 or 50 shekels.)

The Visions.

Very few who lightheartedly embark on prophetic speculation have much idea of the variety and number of the explanations of Daniel that have been seriously put forward by Christian expositors worthy of respect. All too often these explanations are mutually exclusive. It is remarkable, too, how seldom the supporter of one view is won over to another. There is not even much evidence that students of prophecy are drawing gradually nearer to one another in their explanations.

If we were simply to give an outline of our own interpretation, it would for these very reasons be largely waste of time. For a survey of all the principal lines of exposition we lack both space and inclination, so we have contented ourselves with laying down certain general principles which we are convinced must underlie any sound exposition of the visions in Daniel.

(a) Daniel is a book "sealed even to the time of the end" (12: 4, also 12: 9; 8: 19, 26). If we add to this an element of uncertainty about the text, and even more about the exact translation, we shall recognize that every detailed and dogmatic interpretation should be treated with extreme reserve.

(b) Ever since Jerome (A.D. 340–420) there has been a wide degree of general agreement on broad lines of exegesis among expositors, until the rise of modern views. Seeing that we have to do with a "sealed book," this is rather remarkable, and it rather disposes of the argument of some more recent writers that we can now understand the book because we are in the end-time. When that comes, we may reasonably expect something startlingly new.

(c) The one prophecy where unanimity might reasonably be expected, that of the Seventy Weeks (9: 24–27), has produced almost as wide a variety of interpretations, many mutually incompatible, as any other passage in this book. This seems to confirm the note of caution already struck.

(d) This dogmatism comes largely from the certainty with which we can apply some parts of the visions to Antiochus Epiphanes, viz. ch. 8 and the bulk of ch. 11. But Lattey is surely right in principle, when he says, "The full exegetical exposition of the Book of Daniel must take into account, as it were, three historical planes, that of the persecution of Antiochus IV Epiphanes, and of the first and second comings of Christ, our Lord. This is part of the mystery of the book, and is not fully expounded in it . . ."[1] The fact that we can so fully understand the book, when it refers to the past, does not imply that the past has exhausted the meaning of any part of the book, or that the past is a sure guide to the understanding of the book in its future aspect.

(e) The most important thing for the average reader is to discover what the Holy Spirit would have us learn from Daniel for to-day. Though he may get a thrill of awe as he realizes how completely the past has been in God's hand, we may be

[1] Lattey: *The Book of Daniel*, p. vii.

sure that this is not the book's chief value. Still less will it be a purely hypothetical picture of things yet future. We may be sure that the chief purpose of Daniel to-day is to bring strength and comfort to the individual or church faced by apparently overwhelming and irresistible difficulties and opposition. Its picture of God's absolute sovereignty in the crisis of the present and in the yet unveiled future is a guarantee of God's succour for all who trust Him and of His ultimate and complete triumph.

Nebuchadnezzar's Dream (Ch. 2).

The king's dream is not referred to elsewhere in Scripture, nor is any attempt made in Daniel to link it with the visions. Its purpose is not to give Nebuchadnezzar a preview of human history—why should God give this to a heathen king?—but to teach him that God is sovereign in the affairs of men, raising up whom He will, and that at the end of an unspecified time of God's own choosing, He would set up His kingdom on earth (ver. 44f). It is not even stated that each kingdom must immediately follow its predecessor. We need hardly doubt that both comings of our Lord are in view here. It is just because the revelation in the dream is general rather than detailed that no attempts at finding deeper interpretations have ever really carried conviction, except to those who have made them.

The End of World History (Ch. 7).

It is a commonplace of exegesis that the four beasts of this chapter are the same as the four portions of the image in ch. 2. The only evidence for this supposition is the alleged suitability of the symbolic animals. Since, however, the symbolism is found suitable both by the supporters of the old traditional views and also of the modern ones, which make everything in the book end with Antiochus Epiphanes, the argument would seem to be rather weak.

In fact, on the face of it, there is no connexion at all. There is no suggestion that the beasts fight with one another, and certainly none are vanquished and destroyed, for when all is finished, the first three are still in existence (ver. 12), while the fourth has been destroyed by God's action (ver. 11). Everything in this vision gives the impression that we are dealing with the end times.

The R.V. of ver. 9 should be noted. Daniel sees God as an old man, because the form of God in this vision is as symbolic as the beasts themselves. Similarly in ver. 13 the R.V. is correct in rendering "one like unto a son of man." This is symbolic language, for ver. 27 clearly equates him with "the

K

people of the saints of the Most High." The one like a man is a people just as the beasts are. This does not mean that we are to rule out the personal interpretation as well, for to the Jew the people without its Messianic ruler was inconceivable and obviously the ruler received the dominion on behalf of his people. As early as the Book of Enoch (*c.* 100 B.C.) it is already clearly used in a Messianic sense. It is to be noted that in Revelation our Lord is linked both with one like unto a son of man and with the ancient of days (Rev. 1: 13f, R.V.).

The Enemy of the Saints (Ch. 8).

The interpretation of this vision is in large measure given (vers. 19–26), and from this it is clear that in the first place it refers predominantly to the persecution of the Jews by Antiochus Epiphanes. On the other hand there is every reason for supposing that this does not exhaust its meaning, for it is clearly stated that "it belongeth to the appointed time of the end" (ver. 19, R.V.). Such an extension of the prophecy hardly seems to justify the prolonging of the primary interpretation beyond the time of Antiochus Epiphanes. In other words we should look on Antiochus rather as a foreshadowing of him who finally fulfills the vision.

The Messiah the Prince (Ch. 9).

In many ways this is the crucial chapter of Daniel. If indeed we have here a prophecy of Jesus Christ, then Daniel is truly prophetic, and its application is not bounded by the times of Antiochus Epiphanes. The test is the fairer, for while the language of vers. 24–27 is cryptic, it is hardly symbolic.

We believe that any unbiased student—not necessarily a Christian—will agree that the usual modern interpretation is unsatisfactory by any normal canons of interpretation. By referring the prophecy to the time of Antiochus Epiphanes a chronological error of some sixty-five years is created. The command (lit. "word") to restore and to build Jerusalem is Jer. 29: 10—surely a desperate expedient! The anointed one, the prince (lit. "an anointed-prince") in ver. 25 (R.V.) is someone else than the anointed one in ver. 26. In addition much remains without adequate explanation. Beek, a modern, is far fairer, when he says quite candidly that he has not found a satisfactory solution.[1]

On the other hand, it will not be chance that this passage is not referred to in the New Testament. Though its application to our Lord and His work seems clear enough, there is no unanimity, when it comes to detail. This lack of agreement seems to deprive the prophecy of most of its evidential value.

[1] M. A. Beek: *Das Danielbuch*, 1935.

Of less importance is the divergence on the question whether the seventieth week is still future or not. Both views involve us in difficulties of exegesis, and up to the present neither side seems to be able to convince the other.

Far more important are the variant efforts to solve the chronological problems involved. Those that take the seventy weeks as meaning 490 years may be divided into four groups:

(a) Those who begin the period with the twentieth year of Artaxerxes (Neh. 2: 1, 5–8) and who consider the error of something over ten years unimportant.

(b) Those who begin it with the seventh year of Artaxerxes (Ezra 7: 7); while the chronology tallies now, there is nothing in the decree given to Ezra (Ezra 7: 11–26) which makes it fit the language of Dan. 9: 25.

(c) Those who reckon from the same starting point as in (a) but work with "prophetic years" of 360 days. There is an inherent artificiality here that has made the theory unacceptable to the majority.

(d) Those who make the decree of Cyrus (Ezra 1: 2ff) the starting point. Undoubtedly this is the most attractive starting point, but the chronology can only be maintained by rejecting the accepted secular dates and affirming, on the basis of Dan. 9, that the decree of Cyrus was 487 years before the crucifixion instead of about 570 as given by all modern secular histories dealing with the period. This is entirely convincing to the convinced, and to none others.

Yet others assure us that the seventy weeks are *merely* a conventional symbolical round number representing the fulness of time. This is of course possible, though improbable; it does save us a lot of trouble in interpretation, but it reduces an apparently precise prediction into a generalization of relatively small evidential value.

The only reasonable conclusion is that God does not wish our faith to rest on chronological proofs, however marvellous. However close the fulfilment may have been in fact, we must probably allow for a symbolic element in the seventy weeks, though we do not agree that they are solely, or even mainly, symbolic.

The Fortunes of Israel (Chs. 10–12).

How remarkable this vision is can be grasped only by one who has studied ch. 11 with the help of a good commentary. In it we have detailed historical prophecy of a type unique in the Bible. The problem that must face the intelligent reverent reader is not whether God could have so foretold the future, but whether He would have so done. We have come to no definite opinion on the subject, but it is worth noting that

Zockler, Wright and Boutflower (conservatives all) suggest that in the time of Antiochus Epiphanes a genuine prophecy of Daniel's was worked over and paraphrased, thus bringing it into this minute conformity with historical detail. If the book was not considered canonical until after the time of Antiochus, such treatment would have been quite possible.

We do not doubt that this prophecy passes over from Antiochus Epiphanes to the Antichrist, whom in many ways he foreshadows, and so in ch. 12 we pass on over to a picture of the end and of the resurrection. It will be noted that only a resurrection of the very good and the very bad seems to be proclaimed (12: 2). This in itself suggests an early date for the book. In the days of Daniel very little clear teaching about the resurrection existed, but in the second century B.C. the resurrection hope, which was to receive its real certainty in Jesus Christ, had already expanded beyond this point.

The exact functions and powers of the angels mentioned in Daniel cannot be decided from the book itself, nor would it be wise to speculate unduly. The doctrine of the sovereignty of God is Daniel's chief theological interest, and the chief function of the angels is to stress the gulf between God and man.

Additional Note.

Those desiring a modern and scholarly answer to some of the attacks on the sixth century date of *Daniel* can refer to D. J. Wiseman and others, *Notes on Some Problems in the Book of Daniel* (Tyndale Press).

APPENDIX

LAMENTATIONS

THE position of Lamentations in the English Bible is due to the LXX. In the Hebrew Bible it is found in the Writings, as the third of the five *Megillot*, or Rolls (Song of Songs, Ruth, Lamentations, Ecclesiastes, Esther); the order within this small collection is not based on authorship, but on the order in which they are read in the Synagogue during the year at the major feasts and fasts. The English name is derived from the Vulgate. In Hebrew, the book is occasionally called *Qinot, i.e.* Lamentations, but normally *Ekah, i.e.* How—the first word of the 1st, 2nd and 4th lamentation.

The book is composed of five lamentations, or dirges, over the destruction of Jerusalem by Nebuchadnezzar; quite understandably it is read in the Synagogue on the 9th of Ab, when a fast is held in remembrance of the destruction of both the first and the second temple.

Authorship.

The book is anonymous, and it is far from certain that all five poems are by the same writer. Both the LXX and Talmudic tradition ascribe it to Jeremiah, and this has been adopted by both the A.V. and R.V.; we should, however, do better to treat this tradition with reserve. Young sums up the position thus: "In the light of these arguments it seems most likely that Jeremiah did compose Lamentations. Of this, however, we cannot be certain, and it seems best to admit that we do not really know who the author was."[1]

Our insistence on the anonymity of the book comes from no mere scholarly pedantry. It comes rather from the conviction that we show the Holy Spirit no respect, when we go beyond the indications of Scripture itself. There are some traditions, like that of the authorship of the Gospel according to Mark, which are so close to the time involved and so borne out by the evidence of the book, that we do not hesitate to accept them; but this does not apply to the traditions about the Old Testament. We are much safer and more reverent in accepting the anonymity imposed by the Holy Spirit Himself.

There is yet another reason. Whenever we make unprovable assertions about the Bible, however good our motive, we open

[1] Young, p. 334.

149

the door wide to the equally unprovable assumptions of the modernist scholar. The fact that the conservative assumption is considered to be "edifying," and the modernist one the reverse, does not lift the former to a higher plane of legitimacy.

Hebrew Poetry.

Poetry achieves its ends by sublimeness of thought, by the felicitous use of words, by the striking nature of the word images it uses, by its use of metre and other rhythmic devices, and by certain technical devices like alliteration and rhyme.

The sublimeness of Hebrew poetic thought needs no stressing, but translation seldom does justice to the choice of words in the original. In addition, as reference to the R.V. mg. will sometimes, but not always, show, the translators have often been afraid of rendering the poetic images literally as being too strong or too striking for the Western ear. Metre Hebrew undoubtedly had, but doubt as to its exact nature, and still more the dissimilar structure of the two languages makes a metrical translation into English either an inadequate reflexion of the original or unsuited for use in public worship and private devotion. The Metrical Version of the Psalms is seldom good poetry and still seldomer a real picture of the Hebrew.

Hebrew uses a little alliteration and assonance, but never rhyme—the few apparent examples are mere accidents. Its main technical device is parallelism or thought rhythm, which echoes the thought in one metrical line in a second or even third line of the same metrical length (for the *qinah* metre see next section). The echo may be:

(a) A complete repetition of the thought in other words:
But his delight is in the law of the LORD;
And in His law doth he meditate day and night. (Ps. 1 : 2.)

(b) A continuation of the thought:
And he shall be like a tree planted by the streams of water,
That bringeth forth its fruit in its season. (Ps. 1: 3.)

(c) A combination of the literal and metaphorical:
Whose leaf also doth not wither,
And in whatsoever he doeth he shall prosper. (Ps. 1: 3.)

(d) The opposite of the original thought (particularly common in Proverbs:
For the LORD knoweth the way of the righteous:
But the way of the wicked shall perish. (Ps. 1: 6.)

(e) Merely formal; the thought just runs on:
But now shall my head be lifted up
Above mine enemies round about me. (Ps. 27: 6.)

Even in the strictly poetical books we find occasional freedom in the metrical structure, lines being longer or shorter than we might have expected. This is a freedom that goes back to the Canaanite poetry of the fifteenth century B.C. discovered at Ras Shamra, and it persists throughout Biblical literature. In the prophetic books it is used sometimes with such freedom that there may even be doubt whether we are dealing with verse or rhythmic prose.[1]

The Literary Form of Lamentations.

The first four poems are written in the *Qinah*, or dirge metre. In this the normal form of Hebrew poetic parallelism is abandoned. Instead of two or more lines of equal length, we have long lines divided into two unequal parts, the second being shorter than the first. Normally the first half has three beats, the second two. The second half continues and fills out the thought of the first half.

The metre is obscured in the A.V., but the R.V. sets out the long lines, without, however, indicating the break. Exigencies of translation more often than not mask the peculiarity of this metre, though once known it can often be recognized. The effect of the metre may be best seen in Moffatt's translation, though he sometimes achieves it only by considerable freedom in his renderings.

In addition, the first four contain an alphabetic acrostic arrangement. There are 22 letters in the Hebrew alphabet, and so chs. 1, 2, and 4 have 22 verses each, while ch. 3 has 66.

In chs. 1 and 2 each verse has three *Qinah* lines, the first line of each verse beginning with the appropriate letter of the alphabet. As translated by the R.V. the following verses have four lines each, 1: 1, 2, 7; 2: 2, 6, 17 (five), 19, but with the exception of 1: 7 and 2: 19 this is due only to faulty division of lines in the R.V. translation.

Ch. 4 resembles chs. 1 and 2, except that each verse has only two long lines. The four lines of ver. 22 are again due to the faulty division in the R.V.

Metrically ch. 3 is the most complicated. It falls into groups of three verses (indicated by the R.V.) in which *each* verse begins with the same letter of the alphabet. In spite of the greater number of verses, the third poem is obviously the same length as the first two.

Ch. 5 employs normal Hebrew parallelism and contains no acrostic. But since it too has 22 verses, one is tempted to wonder whether the author had intended at some time to transform it into an acrostic poem. Though it is not in the *Qinah* metre, a dirge-like note is struck by the assonances of

[1] For further details see HDB or ISBE, article Poetry, Hebrew.

the endings -u, -nu, -anu, -enu, -inu, -unu no less than 44 times.

It is the extremely artificial nature of the metre employed in these poems that has been one of the chief reasons for making many conservative scholars hesitant to accept the traditional authorship. We are not dealing here with the spontaneous outpourings of a broken heart, but with polished and self-conscious literature. Jeremiah was a great poet, but we find nothing in his prophetic poems to prepare us for Lamentations.

The First Lament.

The first poem deals with the desolation and misery of Jerusalem. The poet speaks in vers. 1–11b, and describes the condition of Jerusalem. Then in vers. 11c–16, Jerusalem herself speaks to Jehovah and recounts the measure of her misery. Her lament is interrupted by the poet with a descriptive verse (ver. 17). Finally Jerusalem closes with a prayer to God (vers. 18–22). As mostly in Lamentations, there is no real note of hope struck. She confesses (ver. 18ff) that her punishment is just; her real hope is that she may see her enemies handled as she has been.

It should be noted that this lament gives the impression of having been written some little time after the destruction of Jerusalem, see especially ver. 7, R.V. Jerusalem's lovers (vers. 2, 19) are the nations she relied on as allies against Babylon.

The Second Lament.

Here we have the undoubted work of an eye-witness of the siege; the lament was probably composed soon after the fall of the city. Its main theme is Jehovah's anger with His people.

In vers. 1–10 we have the casting off by God of people, land and sanctuary. In ver. 9 the A.V., "the law is no more," seems to be more correct than the R.V., though its force might easily be misunderstood. The three groups of leaders, kings and princes, priests, prophets, are being referred to. It is the priestly guidance of life that has come to an end with the destruction of the temple.

In vers. 11–17 he laments the punishment of Jerusalem and describes the callousness of the neighbouring nations. It is not clear whether ver. 11ff look back to the horrors of the siege, or whether they describe the misery of the survivors after the leading citizens had been deported.

In ver. 18f Zion is called to give herself to prayer, and vers. 20ff are her response. Though the tenses in ver. 20 are future, the questions are rhetorical and refer to what had already happened.

The Third Lament.

Though this poem occasionally uses the first person plural, as a whole it is written in the first person singular. It is far from certain whether we have here a description of the author's own experiences, or whether a representative Israelite or even personified Jerusalem is made to speak. On balance the second or third view seems the more probable.

The first twenty verses are a description of personal sufferings. Then the speaker calls to mind that running through all his sufferings there had been the grace of God; otherwise he would have been completely destroyed. This in turn creates hope for the future. So he calls for penitence (vers. 40–54). This leads to new hope (ver. 55ff) and a call to God for vengeance on his enemies (vers. 58–66). It is striking that here, too, the only hope open seems to be rather that his enemies should suffer as he has, than that he should be restored to his old estate.

This lament stands out in sharp contrast with the rest of the book. Were it elsewhere, e.g. among the Psalms, few would think of associating it with the fall of Jerusalem. It is not so much the physical misery of the siege and the shame of captivity and exile that weigh on the poet, as the spiritual misery of being separated from God by a sense of guilt and the destruction of the sanctuary. In many ways it is reminiscent of portions of the book of Job.

The Fourth Lament.

In most respects this poem stands in close relationship to the second. Here, too, there are clear reminiscences of the siege. Its theme is the contrast between Zion past and present.

The first eleven verses present the contrast itself. In ver. 6 the A.V. has missed the point. It is not the punishment of Jerusalem and of Sodom that are being compared, but their iniquity. In ver. 7 the R.V. is probably correct in rendering "nobles" rather than "Nazirites."

The change in Zion's fortunes is then attributed to the sins of the priests and prophets (vers. 12–16) which left no hope of a refuge once the storm broke (vers. 17–20). The "nation that could not save" (ver. 17) is, of course, Egypt. The poet then looks forward to a similar reversal of fate that will come to Zion's foes as personified by Edom (ver. 21ff).

The Fifth Lament.

Fittingly the book closes with an appeal to Jehovah. In the first eighteen verses the poet describes the afflictions of

Jehovah's people, and then ends with the abiding power of God. The closing verse should be rendered as in the R.V. margin:

> Unless thou hast utterly rejected us
> And art very wroth against us.

It is the note of hope, but of subdued hope. To avoid ending the reading of the book on even a qualified minor key, the Synagogue has ver. 21 repeated after ver. 22. Since the generation of the destruction could not plead personal innocence, it looks as though ver. 7 implies a date some time on in the exile for this the last of the poems.

The Messianic Interpretation.

Certain passages are frequently used with reference to the Passion of our Lord. The most obvious are 1: 12 and certain expressions in ch. 3. As long as this is done reverently and knowingly, few would cavil at it. The reason why this is possible is instructive.

Our Lord is the Second Man (I Cor. 15: 47). The sufferings of the righteous before Him were but foreshadowings of His sufferings, and the punishment of sin was a foreshadowing of what He would have to bear when He took our place as our substitute. It is therefore entirely to be expected that in this book of the suffering for sin, there would be the frequent phrase that would remind the loving heart of a much deeper suffering.

The Purpose of Lamentations.

One fallacy that is widely held is that inspiration is a question merely of authorship. For those who held it, the "fact" of Jeremiah's authorship of Lamentations was sufficient justification for its being in the Bible. But the reason why any particular book is included in the Canon of Scripture must be deeper than that.

The Bible sets out to give us every facet of the impact of God's revelation on man. There is no aspect of human life, once it has been brought into the sphere of the operation of God's Spirit, that is not illumined by some book of the Bible.

Grief, great and crushing, is an unavoidable part of human life. Even in the new covenant it can come, and even there it can come as the result of sin, one's own or another's. To one who is passing through such an experience, who feels that the sun can never shine again as it once did, Lamentations may speak its word of comfort in ways that cannot be grasped by those who have not gone down into the vale of grief.

BIBLIOGRAPHY

THOUGH the books given below will tell you much about the prophets, that is not why they have been listed. They have been chosen as books which will help you to understand the text and thought of the prophets more easily. Very few are obtainable new, but most should be in a good public library.

Isaiah

Skinner: The Book of the Prophet Isaiah (C.B.—2 vols.)—preferably the edition of 1915 or later.

G. A. Smith: The Book of Isaiah (2 vols. Expositor's Bible or Hodder & Stoughton).

Jeremiah

Peake: Jeremiah & Lamentations (Century Bible—2 vols.).

Streane: The Book of the Prophet Jeremiah together with the Lamentations (C.B.)—the edition of 1913 or later only recommended.

Ezekiel

Davidson & Streane: The Book of the Prophet Ezekiel (C.B.)—preferably the edition of 1916 or later.

Ellison: Ezekiel: The Man and His Message.

Daniel

Lattey: The Book of Daniel (Browne and Nolan)—this is a volume of the Roman Catholic Westminster Version.

Boutflower: In and Around the Book of Daniel (S.P.C.K.)—it deals fully with most of the difficulties raised against the historicity of the book.

Lang: The Histories and Prophecies of Daniel (Paternoster Press) —probably the sanest modern attempt to explain the visions of Daniel.

The Minor Prophets

G. A. Smith: The Book of the Twelve Prophets (2 vols.—Expositor's Bible or Hodder & Stoughton).

Horton & Driver: The Minor Prophets (Century Bible—2 vols.).

Knight: The Book of Hosea (Torch Commentary).

Driver: The Books of Joel and Amos (C.B.)—preferably the edition of 1915 or later.

Lanchester: Obadiah and Jonah (C.B.).

Davidson & Lanchester: The Books of Nahum, Habakkuk and Zephaniah (C.B.).

Barnes: Haggai, Zechariah and Malachi (C.B.)—edition of 1934 or later.

Baron: The Visions and Prophecies of Zechariah (Morgan & Scott) —the best treatment of the predictive element of Zechariah.

INDEX OF SCRIPTURE PASSAGES

INDEX OF SUBJECTS

(This index does not include those topics entirely or mainly in
the natural position where they occur in the prophetic books.)